Is G
the Homosexual?

R. T. Kendall

Marshall Pickering

Other books by Dr R. T. Kendall

Calvin and English Calvinism to 1649 (OUP)
Jonah (Hodder and Stoughton)
Who By Faith (Hodder and Stoughton)
Tithing (Hodder and Stoughton)
Stand Up and Be Counted (Hodder and Stoughton)
Does Jesus Care? (Hodder and Stoughton)
Once Saved, Always Saved (Hodder and Stoughton)
God Meant it for Good (Kingsway)

Marshall Morgan and Scott
Marshall Pickering
3 Beggarwood Lane, Basingstoke, Hants RG23 7LP, UK

Copyright © 1988 R. T. Kendall
First published in 1988
by Marshall Morgan and Scott Publications Ltd
Part of the Marshall Pickering Holdings Group
A subsidiary of the Zondervan Corporation

British Library CIP Data

Kendall, R. T.
    Is God for the homosexual?
    1. Homosexuality – Religious aspects –
    Christianity
    I. Title
    261.8'35766   BR115.H6

    ISBN 0-551-01600-0

Text set in Baskerville by Brian Robinson, Buckingham
Printed in Great Britain by Anchor Brendon Ltd,
Colchester, Essex.

Contents

To John

'Parliament isn't the great institution of life. Churches are your great institutions, as are your great voluntary associations. And you're entitled to look to them and say, "Look, there are certain standards and if you undermine fundamentally these standards you'll be changing our way of life." When the authority of those institutions is undermined because they haven't been forthright, it is then that people turn too much to the State.'

So, she thinks the churches should be more outspoken on the subject of AIDS?

'I think so, yes. To do them justice some of them have been forthright.'

Margaret Thatcher Interview, *Woman's Own*
(31st October 1987)

'Dr Kendall's approach rests upon the fact that, in the Bible when God reveals His Law He accompanies it with the promise of Grace, by which we can be forgiven and enabled joyfully to obey His Will: this book is therefore both realistic about sin and its effects and full of hope in that it offers the true compassion which springs from the Gospel of Christ.'

Dr Graham Leonard
Bishop of London

'Christians too often find it easier to love their enemies than homosexuals they do not even know; but in this gracious book Dr Kendall succeeds in placing side by side his uncompromising opposition to the sin with his equally uncompromising friendship for the sinner. It reminds me of Jesus, and that poor sinful woman they wanted to stone.'

Dr Nigel Cameron
Warden of Rutherford House
Edinburgh

'We have heard much from doctors, social workers and educationalists on the issue of homosexuality. Now at last a theologian speaks out and with devastating effects. R T Kendall does not pull his punches and the results are well worth reading.'

Rev Clive Calver
General Secretary
Evangelical Alliance

Preface

In 1986 I began a series of sermons in Westminster
Chapel from Romans 1 under the theme 'The God
of the Bible'. In early 1987 I was invited by Dr Nigel
Cameron, Warden of Rutherford House, Edinburgh, to deliver a lecture at Westminster Central
Hall on the subject 'AIDS: is it God's Judgement?'
Had I not been forced to research this question I am
sure that I would not have been at all ready for my
treatment of Romans 1:26, 27.

I turned to Dr Gaius Davies, a consultant in the
Department of Psychological Medicine at King's
College Hospital, for advice. He graciously spent
time with me and also put me in touch with
considerable literature on both AIDS and homosexuality. I cannot sufficiently thank him for his
kindness.

The Rev Lyndon Bowring, Chairman of Care
Trust, offered invaluable suggestions as I worked
through the difficult question of AIDS and God's
judgement. Dr Patrick Dixon, author of *The Truth
About AIDS* (Kingsway, 1987) has also been a
productive source. The quote by him at the
beginning of Chapter Five is not found in his book
but was a 'throw away' remark he made to me

recently over dinner. *Beyond AIDS* (Kingsway), written by my friend The Rev Gavin Reid, unfortunately did not reach me in time to incorporate into my own book.

It never crossed my mind that my sermons on Romans 1:26, 27 would become a book. This therefore explains some repetition. I hope the reader will also keep in mind that I do not pose as an expert in either homosexuality or AIDS. My interest was and is entirely theological and that which will lead to the salvation of souls. I was therefore pleased that Mrs Christine Whittell of Marshall Pickering asked to make these sermons into a book. I have enjoyed working with her and do appreciate the interest she has taken.

I express my warmest thanks to Mrs Doris Midgley, Mrs Jackie Heather and Mrs Diana Williams, each of whom has had a hand in either the typing or the re-typing of the manuscript.

When I told him I planned to quote from the immortal hymn by F W Faber (1814–63) in the context of God's judgement, Dr Davies assumed that I knew that the author was a non-practising homosexual. But this was news to me. He showed me this in Geoffrey Faber's book *Oxford Apostles*. All this adds up to a lovely irony which is quite relevant for the present time and it is in this spirit that I commit the book to the reader:

'There's a wideness in God's mercy
Like the wideness of the sea:
There's a kindness in his justice,
Which is more than liberty.'

R T Kendall

London
January 1988

8

Introduction

When I announced to my church I would be preaching a series of sermons on 'AIDS and homosexuality' many of us prayed that God would give us an undoubted conversion from the homosexual community. I had never preached on this subject before. I felt out of my depth. But I felt none the less that I had to tackle the subject. And yet I had to ask myself, 'Why am I doing this? Why am I really preaching on this?'

It seemed to me that if someone were not converted as a result of my talks there would follow a sense of futility. Not that such an emphasis was not needed in this day and age; but surely, if Jesus Christ is the 'same yesterday, today and forever' (Heb. 13:8), we should expect to see his power displayed before our very eyes.

In the meantime we raised over £2,500 to buy advertising at appropriate Underground stations. We used the theme 'Is there hope in the Age of AIDS?' Answer: Yes. We had reason to believe a good number of people came along to our Sunday evening services as a direct result of those ads.

After my first sermon of that series a young man came into my vestry. He introduced himself as a leader of the Gay Rights Movement. Seeing the advertisements in Victoria Station, he decided to come along and see what we were up to. He was not happy with my stand on homosexual practice but he kindly said that he was surprised at one thing, that I cared. He sensed a compassionate spirit in my approach, and this encouraged me. For that is precisely what I wanted any homosexual person to sense. He promised to keep coming, but I never saw him again.

During that series I welcomed more people, as far as I know, of the Gay community than at any time during my ten years in London. All of them were kind and gracious to me.

Save for one. John. His first appearance at Westminster Chapel came on the evening of May 24th 1987 when my subject was 'AIDS: God's Judgement?' (see Chapter 5). He was so angry, he said, that he felt he must come in and give me a piece of his mind for preaching such rubbish. He said that I must be the most dangerous man in London for uttering such nonsense publicly. I must be stopped. He left in a rage.

To my surprise, John came back the following Sunday night. He came into the vestry. His attitude was totally different. But he still wanted to say, 'I could have killed you last Sunday night.' And yet I could tell something had begun to happen to him. 'I've got to say that you are absolutely right in everything you said last week. Everything. But I don't know what to do. I have been living with a man for twelve years, since I was 18 years old.'

I saw before my eyes a classic case of conviction of sin. The Holy Spirit had seized him. What was I to do? I knew the church was praying for someone like him to be converted. Was I really ready for this, not to mention the pastoral responsibility in the months ahead?

I knew what I had to do. He had just heard my preaching of the Gospel (see Chapter 6). He was like a ripe fruit waiting to be plucked. I went over the Gospel with him one more time. I asked if he understood the implications. He said that he did. I then asked if he wanted to receive Jesus Christ as his Lord and Saviour. He said that He did. We prayed together. I led him to Christ.

When we finished praying he looked at me with an electrifying smile. 'I feel brilliant,' he said, 'I feel absolutely brilliant. And I know I am going to Heaven.'

We talked a while longer. He had not seen the advertisements in Victoria. One of our Pilot Lights (those who witness on the streets on Saturdays) had given him a tract. That had brought him to our church. He also said that he had quit sleeping with his friend after the previous Sunday night sermon (despite his anger).

Things have been far from easy for John since his remarkable conversion. The break-up with his friend, with whom he had consented to a homosexual marriage in Las Vegas two years before, was unpleasant. He got little encouragement from his parents when he told them of his becoming a Christian. His father was so upset that he regarded John's Christianity as being 'worse than gay'. On top of that, he resigned his job as an airline steward and has had considerable difficulty in getting another job.

It has been 'a total nightmare since being a Christian,' John told me recently. 'But I can't turn back. I'd die. Life wouldn't be worth carrying on.' And yet he says that his former life had been 'so perfect in my own mind.' But 'when I know I am born again I stop dead in my tracks.' At the same time he confesses, 'all you see in your life looks so bleak. Some days you feel you have the Holy Spirit and you feel fantastic. The next day he seems gone. Pinch me, it was just a bad dream. But even if it was a dream I'd still search for God because the dream opened my eyes to so many things I'd have to seek the Lord anyway. But I'm glad it's not a dream.'

I have quoted the above verbatim lest anybody who thinks about becoming a Christian will fancy the new way of life 'a flowery bed of roses'. It is not that. Jesus said, 'If any man will come after me, let him deny himself, and take up his cross, and follow me (Matt. 16:24).

God's way is the best way to live. What is more, this life is not all there is. That is why I have stressed the age to come – the Bible calls it 'eternity' – that we might see afresh ultimately why Jesus died for us. I'm glad it's not a dream.

Chapter One

Lowering our Voices

Why write on this subject? There are several reasons. First, we are all aware of the AIDS epidemic. Public awareness of this disease – and its spread – are far from being at their peak, and I have no doubt that one year from now all I will be saying will be even more relevant. And we cannot know what things will be like ten years from now. What we do know at the present time is that approximately seventy-five per cent of those who have AIDS are homosexuals, and as a result, AIDS has been called, even if unfairly, the Gay Plague.

Before I go any further I think I should define certain terms. Let us be clear what we are talking about. A homosexual is a person who has a sexual desire for the same sex; a man wanting another man, a woman desiring another woman. If it is a man he is usually called Gay. If it is a women she is called Lesbian.

The heterosexual is one who has a desire for the opposite sex; man with woman, woman with man. Heterosexual monogamy is the basis of Christian marriage. Monogamy refers to having but one single partner. The Biblical view of marriage is monogamous, one partner of the opposite sex within marriage bonds.

A bisexual is one who has a desire for either sex. This desire fluctuates, depending on the situation of the person, for he can commit the sex act with someone of either sex. This is how AIDS spreads so easily into the heterosexual community, that is, by a bisexual person who has previously committed the sex act with a homosexual who has the HIV virus (to be explained below). Thus the same bisexual person may later have intercourse with a woman and give her the HIV virus. Another man has a sexual relationship with her, gets the virus, and spreads it on and on into the heterosexual community.

The asexual is someone whose sexual desire is either indeterminate or with virtually no sex drive at all.

The second reason I wish to write on this subject is that we are more and more aware of the legalisation of homosexuality in Britain today. In 1967 Parliament passed the Sexual Offences Act, after accepting the Wolfenden Report of 1957. This report recommended that consenting men over twenty-one be permitted to engage in sexual acts in private. As a result, such acts were no longer regarded as a crime. Now here we need to make a distinction between *crime* and *sin*. Crime is breaking the social law. Sin is breaking the law of God. So as a result of the 1967 Act, private homosexual practice between consenting men is no longer a crime – but that does not mean that such practice is not still a sin. It is likely that many MPs or Peers would never have passed that Bill had they known it was going to result in a nationwide Charter for Gay Rights, with such practices eventually being advocated in some schools as acceptable behaviour. Many voted for the bill only in order to neutralise a situation in which certain prominent persons were at risk of blackmail by unscrupulous men.

The third reason for writing on this subject is that we are very much aware of the efforts of some to dignify this practice which was once regarded as shameful. There are those who are not content with the Law of 1967. They have taken this Bill to give them what they believe is their right not only to publicise their behaviour, but to dignify it. This kind of thinking has become widespread, and many – not all of whom are even Gays or Lesbians – now press for the acceptance of homosexual practice as an equally valid option.

Many of the MPs and Peers who voted for the 1967 Bill nevertheless stated that homosexual practice was unnatural – and they regarded it as such. But over the last ten or fifteen years the propaganda of the Gay Movement has called it natural. The former Greater London Council sponsored the Gay and Lesbian Charter (whose Foreword was written by Ken Livingstone) which recommends, among other things, that police protection should be removed from people or bodies who speak publicly against homosexual practice, and that charitable status should also be removed from churches or organisations which oppose such practice.

The fourth but main reason for dealing with this subject is because of what the Bible says on the matter. Paul in Romans 1:26–27 calls the practice of homosexuality 'against nature'. 'For this cause God gave them up into vile affections; for even their women did change the natural use into that which is against nature: And likewise also the men, leaving the natural use of the woman, burned in their lust one

15

toward another; men with men working that which is unseemly, and receiving in themselves that recompense of their error which was meet' (Rom. 1:26, 27). You will notice the reference to women, ' . . . for even their women did change the natural use into that which is against nature'. The 1967 Act which I have referred to does not refer to Lesbians, but only to homosexual men. Romans 1:26 is the only verse in the Bible which refers explicitly to Lesbian practice.

Now before I go further there are certain distinctions which need to be made. We need to be quite clear about one very important distinction; the difference between homosexual *proclivity* and homosexual *practice*. Proclivity simply refers to one's own inclination or desire. So homosexual proclivity is a desire for one's own sex. And it must be stated here that there are many, many people who have such a desire but who would never dream of carrying out the actual practice. Just as there are heterosexual people who would not dream of committing adultery or engaging in pre-marital sex.

But homosexual practice is more than just proclivity. It is giving in to the temptation to engage in sex acts with one's own sex – whether one is Gay or Lesbian. And it must be said that to have an inclination – a proclivity towards the same sex is *not* a sin, and such should not be regarded as sinful. That a man does not desire woman and is tempted by another man does not in itself make him a sinner, and a person is not to be condemned. There is a difference between temptation and sin. As the hymn puts it, 'Yield not to temptation, for yielding is sin.'

I realise that to quote the Bible nowadays is to

sound like a 'voice crying in the wilderness'. Those who champion Gay Rights have had such momentum on their side in the last several years, that when you quote the Bible it is laughed at, ridiculed, even hated more than ever. For that reason, if a homosexual should be converted in an age such as this – if he is converted to Jesus Christ and renounces his sinful ways – it will be a stunning testimony indeed to the grace of God. For everything is working against us and the message I am putting forward in this book is one which is not often heard. And if you are reading this book – perhaps by accident, perhaps someone gave this to you – and you are a practising homosexual and justify your desire, you may be feeling quite hostile at the moment. So obviously if a person like you were to be converted it would be something beyond your grasp. Only God could do it.

And yet that's the way it is with anybody. Anyone who is a Christian did not become a Christian because he thought 'naturally' that it was the right thing to do. He didn't say, 'Ah, this turns me on, I'll become a Christian.' To become a Christian is an act of the Holy Spirit. Whether one is homosexual, heterosexual, bisexual or asexual – we are *all* equally sinners in the sight of God. The Bible says 'All have sinned, and come short of the glory of God' (Rom. 3:23).

Therefore if you should be one of those who is being described acutely in this book, and you feel self-conscious or that you're being put on the spot, you ought to know that no one intends to single you out. For you, in fact, are *no different* from anyone else as far as being a 'sinner' is concerned. All of us have sinned and come short of the glory of God. For the person who is happily married and even faithful to his wife or her husband still needs to be converted by the grace of God. There are people who are perfectly moral and who would not even think of having sexual practice outside of marriage who are equally lost and on the road to hell.

Jesus said, 'The son of man is come to seek and to save that which was lost' (Luke 19:10). So whoever you are, as you read this – whether heterosexual or homosexual – the only way you can ever be converted by the God of the Bible is to come to see yourself as lost. This means that you must come to the place where you stop justifying yourself. You must stop saying, 'Well this is the way I am made and I can't help it. I must have gratification – surely God understands that.' What I invite you to do is to lower your voice and ask yourself the question, 'What does God say about all this?'

So I want us to see what the Bible does say. You should know that homosexuality as such is dealt with explicitly nine times in the Bible[1], and implicitly at various other times. The first verse I would like to quote is from Leviticus 18:22. The Authorised Version reads: 'Thou shalt not lie with mankind as with womankind: it is an abomination.' The same passage from the NIV makes the meaning just a little more clear, 'Do not lie with a man as one lies with a woman: that is detestable.' I now quote Leviticus 20:13. The AV reads 'If a man also lie with mankind, as he lieth with a woman, both of them have committed an abomination: they shall surely be put to death; their blood shall be upon them.' Again, the NIV reads, 'If a man lies with a man as one lies with a woman, both of them have done what is detestable. They must be put to death;

their blood will be on their own heads.' This gives you a fairly strong hint of what the God of the Bible thinks about the practice of homosexuality.

In Romans 1:26, 27 we have already seen the reference to both Lesbianism and male homosexuality. Such practice is 'against nature'. In 1 Corinthians 6:9–11, there is a reference to the effeminate (the NIV translates this bluntly as the 'pervert'), 'Be not deceived: neither fornicators, nor idolaters, nor adulterers, nor effeminate, nor abusers of themselves with mankind . . . shall inherit the kingdom of God.' Paul refers to this again in 1 Timothy 1:9, 10, 'Know this, that the law is not made for the righteous man, but . . . for sinners, for unholy and profane . . . for whoremongers, for them that *defile themselves with mankind*' (NIV: 'perverts').

In Genesis Chapter 19, we read about the destruction of Sodom and Gomorrah. This provides the first mention in the Bible of homosexual practice, and the expression sodomy – which is a way of referring to homosexual intercourse – comes from this story. There are those in the so-called Gay Christian Movement who have wanted to dismiss this account. Some have even gone so far as to say it is not referring to sex at all. But such an attitude only shows how much one may desire to ignore what is in the Bible.

Now the story is this, quoting the NIV, 'Two angels arrived in Sodom in the evening. And Lot was sitting in the gateway of the city when he saw them. He got up to meet them and bowed down with his face to the ground. "My Lords," he said, "please turn aside to your servant's house. You can wash your feet and spend the night and then go on your way early in the morning." "No," they answered, "we will spend the night in the square." But he insisted so strongly that they did go with him and entered his house. He prepared a meal for them baking bread without yeast, and they ate. Before they had gone to bed, all the men from every part of the city of Sodom, both young and old, surrounded the house. They called to Lot, "Where are the men who came to you tonight? Bring them out to us so that we can have sex with them." Lot went outside to meet them, and shut the door behind him and said, "No, my friends. Don't do this wicked thing. Look, I have two daughters who have never slept with a man. Let me bring them out to you, and you can do what you like with them. But don't do anything to these men, for they have come under the protection of my roof."

"Get out of the way," they replied. And they said, "This fellow came here as an alien, and now he wants to play judge! We'll treat you worse than them." They kept bringing pressure on Lot and moved forward to break down the door.'

It is at this point that the angel of God stepped in. Lot and his family were spared. But you can see this awful situation, which showed not only the proclivity and the practice but also the promiscuity of homosexuality.

This, moreover, was in Sodom and Gomorrah, cities which would be regarded as *outside* the realm of God's covenant people. But now I want to refer to the book of Judges Chapter 19, because this incident took place right in Israel! It is one thing to have the practice of sodomy in the world, but another when it becomes something which takes place among those who are the professing people of God.

In Judges Chapter 19 beginning at verse 22, we read (NIV): 'While they were enjoying themselves some of the wicked men of the city surrounded the house. Pounding on the door, they shouted to the old man who owned the house, "Bring out the man who came to your house so we can have sex with him." The owner of the house went outside and said to them, "No, my friends, don't be so vile. Since this man is my guest, don't do this disgraceful thing. Look, here is my virgin daughter, and his concubine. I will bring them out to you, now, and you can use them and do to them whatever you wish. But to this man don't do such a disgraceful thing." '

What is so disgraceful in this case is that such a thing was taking place among the professing people of God. For what often happens is this. If the church – the professing people of God – do not have an unequivocal stand and do not have a voice which is heard and received in the nation, eventually sin will not only be commonplace in the nation but in the Church as well. And it is a sad fact that this sin is something which has crept right into the Church. And the time has come when the people of God must stand up and be counted, and call a spade a spade. There is only one word for homosexual practice – and that is sin. We are in a meloncholy era indeed when churchmen give the impression that adultery is 'sin' but homosexual practice is but 'less than ideal'. Whoever you are, even if you are a practising homosexual, please do not justify yourself because you have got the current tide on your side. For the same God who once destroyed Sodom and Gomorrah will have the last word in our generation too. And I come to you with Christian compassion; don't be a fool and play fast and loose with your one and only soul. Because this life is not all there is. 'For what shall it profit a man, if he shall gain the whole world, and lose his own soul? Or what shall a man give in exchange for his soul' (Mark 8:36, 37).

As for those who have got AIDS, and know they have got only months to live, they are none the less people who have the opportunity to get right with God. And it may be that some of them will call upon the name of the Lord, people who otherwise may have lived a normal length of years and be lost.

However much one says his drive must be satisfied, it *can* be controlled. And not only that – the power of Christ is sufficient to give one deliverance from the practice. Some are delivered not only from the practice but also from the proclivity. I don't say this happens with all – but in some who have made a one hundred and eighty degree turn in their lifestyles the natural desire for women has been restored. Some have got married and had children. This is what the power of Christ can do.

Although the Bible calls this homosexual practice an 'abomination', it is not the only thing the Bible calls by that name. According to Proverbs 6:16–19, our pride, the sin of lying and the sin of gossip are also an abomination! I quote this because of any self-righteous insensitive church members who know no sympathy and who may be reading these lines. Are you against the homosexual? God is for the homosexual. Perhaps up to now you have been thinking 'I'm glad he's giving it to them'. Well, listen to Proverbs 6:16–19, 'These six things doth the Lord *hate*: yea, seven are an *abomination* unto him: A proud look, a lying tongue, and hands that shed innocent blood. An heart that deviseth wicked imaginations,

22

feet that be swift in running to mischief, a false witness that speaketh lies, and he that soweth discord among brethren.' So don't you dare point a finger, because in your pointing you too have become what is described right here – an abomination in the sight of God.

We who are part of the professing Christian Church must be cleansed of three things. Firstly – of the idea that the homosexual is irrevocably cursed of God. Because this is just not so. The apostle Paul said this when he wrote to the church at Corinth, 'Know ye not that the unrighteous shall not inherit the kingdom of God? Be not deceived: neither fornicators, nor idolaters, nor adulterers, nor effeminate, nor abusers of themselves with mankind, nor thieves, nor covetous, nor drunkards, nor revilers, nor extortioners, shall inherit the kingdom of God. And such were some of you . . . ' (v 9–11). Here described are those who were obviously homosexual and who were converted. So away with the notion that the homosexual is cursed of God! God can save anybody. We are all sinners.

We need, secondly, as members of the Church of Jesus Christ, to be cleansed from that which is now being called 'homophobia'. John Stott defines this as 'an irrational fear or hatred of, even a revulsion' towards the Gay or Lesbian person. Thus one treats a homosexual much like the leper was treated in the time of Jesus. Why should we act like that? Perhaps some have to affirm their own virility or piety to themselves! Well, that is not right. Would that be the attitude of Jesus? Most certainly not. We are told that Jesus was a High Priest who was 'touched with the feeling of our infirmities' (our weaknesses). Jesus was '*in all points* tempted like as we are, yet without sin' (Heb. 4:15).

Jesus understands any weakness that we have. So well does he understand and sympathise, that if you cannot find a single other person in this world to sympathise with your plight, your tendency and your weakness – I want you to know that Jesus understands and that he accepts you. If you are homosexual, I am not asking you to listen to some church members. For some of them may have given you a voice of self-righteousness and put you right off. I am asking you, to listen to Jesus Christ, who says to you, whoever you are, 'Come unto me, all you that labour and are heavy laden, and I will give you rest' (Matt. 11:28). Jesus knows that you do feel guilty. No doubt you have got some comfort from the fact that the Gay Rights Movement is getting a momentum and that there are those who are championing your position. But that doesn't deal with your guilt, does it? You feel pretty awful inside.

There is a third attitude from which I would urge the Church to be cleansed; a patronising attitude towards the homosexual. None of us wants to be patronised. I can tell you right now that if I have difficulty with anything in this world, it is someone patronising me. When I sense that, I have to pray for 'double' grace, because I cannot bear it! And I can imagine how homosexual people might sometimes feel. Jesus was never patronising, that is, he never gave out the impression that he was better than or above those who needed him – whatever their condition. We never help anyone for whom we feel a patronising attitude. The apostle Paul said, 'Brethren, if a man be overtaken in a fault, ye which are spiritual, restore such an one in the spirit of meekness; considering thyself, lest thou also be tempted' (Gal. 6:1).

Before I close this chapter I want to say this. There is a reason why Paul could describe homosexuals who had come to Christ in the way he did in 1 Corinthians 6. It is because they themselves came to know that they *needed* cleansing. For all who have sinned want to feel clean, to know that all of their sins were washed away. The Psalmist said, 'As far as the east is from the west, so far hath he removed our transgressions from us' (Ps. 103:13). Let me explain what that means.

Jesus Christ of Nazareth was the God-man. That means he was God as though he were not man – he was man as though he were not God. A great mystery! A glorious truth! Jesus was God in the flesh. But on Good Friday wicked people took Jesus of Nazareth and nailed spikes through his hands against a slab of wood. They hoisted this wood up in the air and dropped it into a hole in the ground, and for six hours Jesus was suspended in the air on the cross. And all the while blood dripped from his hands and his feet and his forehead, where earlier they had put a crown of thorns. And those seeing that blood dripping would not have had a clue at the time that they were looking at the most precious commodity in the history of the human race. The blood of Jesus. More precious than gold. More precious than diamonds. The money that was spent last year on the Duchess of Windsor's jewels would not even remotely begin to come close to the value of that blood which dripped from the God-man on the cross. Because that blood was actually crying out to God, 'Let your justice be satisfied.' And God's justice *was* satisfied.

During that time Jesus himself couldn't understand why the Father turned his back on him, and he cried out, 'My God, my God, why hast thou forsaken me?' (Matt. 27:46). But just before he died Jesus uttered the words, 'It is finished.' And do you know – they have discovered that the words, 'it is finished' are the English translation of a Greek phrase *Tetelestai*, which was a colloquial expression of the ancient marketplace. And it meant 'Paid in full'. Jesus knew that the Father was satisfied by the blood that he shed, so that when he died, your debt and mine was paid.

And what I call on you to do right now is to stop justifying yourself. Transfer the hope you have had in yourself, or in your good works (for I'm sure you have a lot of good works) to Jesus' blood. Whoever you are – whether an adulterer, or a thief, or a gossip or one who has been practising homosexuality – we all need this cleansing. If you will just put 'all your eggs into one basket' – transfer your hope in yourself to what Jesus did for you and believe that he has paid your debt – you can be set free.

[1]Genesis 19: 1–11; Leviticus 18:22 and 20:13; Judges 19:22–25; Romans 1:25–27; 1 Corinthians 6:9–11; 1 Timothy 1:9–10; 2 Peter 2:6–7; Jude 7.

Chapter Two

Is God Against the Homosexual?

We must look again at Romans 1:26, 27, for these verses are particularly relevant for the present time. Paul says, 'For this cause God gave them up into vile affections; for even their women did change the natural use into that which is against nature. And likewise also the men, leaving the natural use of the woman, burned in their lust one toward another; men with men, working that which is unseemly, and receiving in themselves that recompense of their error which was meet.'

Now all of us are aware of the AIDS epidemic. I am sure that this chapter, and what I will say throughout this book, will be even more relevant one year from now, not to mention five years from now. For we are on the brink of one of the worst epidemics – you could even say disasters, in the history of the world[1].

It is well known that most of those who have AIDS are homosexuals. Rightly or wrongly, AIDS has been called the Gay Plague. Now these words of Paul in Romans refer to homosexual practice and there is no way you can read these verses and think that God approves of homosexual practice. But in the last fifteen to twenty years a shift has taken place in public thinking, so that what was once thought to be shameful and disgraceful is now dignified and encouraged. In some places, even, it is not only taught as an equally valid sexual preference, but it is implied that it is even better.

It is our task to deal with what the Bible has to say, and I wish to do so in a loving, non-judgemental way. We are going to combine our Biblical material with what has been generally accepted by medical people and psychologists – some of whom are Christian and some of whom are not. We cannot ignore the contribution made by modern studies which have attempted to understand homosexuality without condoning it.

Now our purpose is threefold, and the first aim is to increase understanding, even sympathy, for the non-practising homosexual. Many Christians have failed here, and have failed miserably. Many of us who are part of the Church have alienated people for whom Christ died and whom Jesus would have accepted.

Now there are two principles which will need looking into here. The first is, that all behaviour has a cause, and the second is that every person is worth understanding. It is so easy for us to be turned off by someone just because we don't understand them. But all behaviour is (in some sense) caused. I want us to look into the question, how much are we what we are because of childhood experiences? I suggest there is truth in the saying, 'As the twig is bent, so is the tree.' Every person is worth understanding and, as far as this subject is concerned, I repeat that we must be cleansed of the phenomenon known as homophobia, irrational fear or hatred of, even a revulsion toward, the homosexual.

The second purpose of this chapter is to assure the

homosexual, without being patronising, that he is loved and accepted by God. There is not one shred of evidence in the Bible that homosexual proclivity signifies the special judgement of God on a person – that God is especially angry with him or her because of a tendency to homosexuality. Because there is an essential difference between homosexual proclivity and homosexual practice, and it is the latter which the Bible condemns.

But the Bible also condemns adultery in exactly the same way. There are those who love to quote Leviticus Chapter 20, verse 13, 'If a man also lie with mankind, as he lieth with a woman, both of them have committed an abomination: they shall surely be put to death.' That is the punishment which was meted out by the Law of Moses in the Old Testament because of what God thought of homosexual practice. But you ought to know that in the same chapter – in verse 10 – it says exactly the same thing about adultery, 'And the man that committeth adultery with another man's wife, even he that committeth adultery with his neighbour's wife, the adulterer and the adulteress shall surely be put to death.' So if you think that homosexual practice is singularly condemned by God, you are wrong. It is condemned, but it is not the only sin. Adultery is abhorred by God as much as homosexual practice. But remember, again, that there is a difference between proclivity – which is a tendency towards – and practice. It is the practice which the Bible condemns, because there is a difference between temptation and sin.

But the third reason for this chapter – indeed, this book – is to motivate the homosexual or Lesbian to come to Christ. You need to know that this Jesus who accepts you completely as you are, died for you on the cross and shed his blood because of your sins. And mine. The Bible says that 'all have sinned, and come short of the glory of God' (Rom. 3:23), so I am not pointing a finger at you. I'm a sinner – we are all sinners – there is no exception.

Jesus is the Son of God. This means he had no earthly father. A virgin named Mary, who lived in Nazareth, had a special visit by Gabriel the angel, who looked at her and said, 'Hail, thou art highly favoured . . . blessed art thou among women' (Luke 1:28). And he gave her the prophecy that she would give birth to a son. And when she said, 'How shall this be, seeing I know not a man?' the angel replied, 'The Holy Ghost shall come upon thee . . . therefore also that holy thing which shall be born of thee shall be called the Son of God' (Luke 1:35). So Mary consented to this, and God implanted her womb with Jesus, who was the God-man; man as though he were not God, God as though he were not man. He was 'at all points tempted like as we are' (Heb. 4:15), so that he understands what I or your friends may not. Your mother or your father may not understand, and he will not laugh at you. He will not scold you or demoralise you. He will accept you.

Jesus went to die on the cross. And when he was on the cross all of our sins – sins we remember, sins we have forgotten, all of them – were put on him as though he were guilty. It is amazing, isn't it? He who knew no sin was made sin (2 Cor. 5:21). And God punished Jesus for what we have done. And all God asks of us is that we affirm his Word and that we don't justify ourselves, but admit that the Bible got it right. This means that you acknowledge that you are a sinner. But you are not a worse sinner than anybody else. We have all sinned.

So I hope that as a consequence of this book you will want to come to Jesus. Which is why I come to you and plead, do not give in to sexual temptation, however great you feel the urge is – because you will suffer the consequences. The consequences of sin are inevitable – and it's just not worth it.

I will deal below with the question of whether AIDS is a judgement of God. But I just want to say this now. AIDS has emerged in our generation, but there is one thing which we all know; that if everybody would just live by the standards of the Bible, there would be no need to fear AIDS. And the Bible says that the only justifiable sex is between a man and a woman within the marriage bonds. In other words – heterosexual monogamy.

I plead therefore that you resist the temptation and do not give in to sin and suffer the consequences. Seek instead God's own revealed will for your life. I make you a promise. Follow what I am saying, and I guarantee that you will be given immense peace. Whoever you are, I want you to know that there is hope. It is the devil who wants you to believe there is no hope – that you cannot ever be different from the way you are. That is the devil's lie.

Now there is a good deal of literature on the subject of homosexuality, and I have read some of it. I have spent a lot of my time reading nothing but psychological and medical books and articles. I will deal with what I believe is most pertinent. Most of the studies which are available deal with male homosexuality more than with Lesbianism.

But Paul, in Romans 1:26, 27 begins with an explicit reference to Lesbianism, the only reference in the Bible to this practice. He says, 'Even their women did change the natural use into that which is against nature.' Now why does Paul, at the beginning of a list of sins which are going to be dealt with throughout Romans 1, mention homosexual practice first? The answer is not because there is a hierarchy of *sin*, but because there is a hierarchy of *shame*. Some have thought that homosexuality is the worst kind of sin, but that it just not true. But it is at the top of the list because of its shame.

Paul had been talking about creation, in Romans 1:20. He said, 'For the invisible things of him from the creation of the world are clearly seen, being understood by the things that are made.' He was discussing the created order. And what did God say in Genesis 1 about man that he had created? 'Male and female created he them' (Gen 1:27). This is the way man was originally made; male and female. And this is the first thing that we need to see clearly; the Bible got it right. It was essential to the creation of man that mankind should be male and female – and the purpose of this was (1) relational (to deal with man's loneliness) and (2) conceptional (to populate the earth). In other words, heterosexual monogamy; man and woman in the marriage bond, where there is fulfilment and procreation. That is God's way.

Now the most common argument used by those who are homosexual is to say, 'Don't tell me homosexuality is unnatural, because it's natural to me.' At this point we have to make the important distinction between what is objectively natural – that is, what the Bible says, and subjectively natural, which is the way one may feel.

The only way one will ever be converted by the Holy Spirit is that he or she comes to affirm that the

Bible got it right; that God created man male and female (Gen. 1:27). This is what is meant by natural. That is the natural order of God's creation. What may 'feel' natural but which is against the natural order of creation is to be ascribed to sin, which is unnatural, and not to God's creation. God did not create man sinful. What is against nature then, is sinful. And so homosexual practice is unnatural because it goes against nature. What is objectively natural is man with woman.

But there is another reason why Paul lists homosexuality first in Romans 1. It is because he has also been talking about the conscience. Romans 1:20 (quoted above) goes on to say, 'so that they are without excuse.' For verse 19 says, 'That which may be known of God is manifest in them; for God hath shewed it unto them.' Paul knows what you in your heart know, that one cannot begin engaging in homosexual activity without feeling pretty awful. However natural it may seem to you, Paul knows, and you know, that a troubled conscience is inevitable. You may begin by telling yourself there's nothing wrong with it, and you may reach the place where it no longer bothers you.

Psychologically, this is called repression – because you have pushed your real feelings down into your subconscious by telling yourself it is all right. But we are made in such a way that when we push something down and deny what we really feel, something else will pop up. It may return as high blood pressure. It may be ill health. It may be all manner of irritable feelings. But it will be basically great guilt, and you won't get away with it. And the result is often what the psychologists call a reaction formation. This is when one 'protests too much', as

Shakespeare put it. This is what has happened in the Gay Rights Movement, which has come along in our generation to encourage one to glory in his or her homosexuality. The Gay Rights Movement has intellectualised this lifestyle. They have virtually turned it into a dogma, as the philosophers did in ancient Greece and claimed it to be the height of bliss. But this is deceitful and absolutely false propaganda. Paul says at the end of verse 27, 'men with men working that which is unseemly, and receiving in themselves that recompense (that is, reward) of their error which was meet.' 'Men committed indecent acts with other men, and received in themselves the due penalty for their perversion' (Romans 1:27b). Does it surprise you then, to learn that this is a reference to ancient diseases which broke out as a consequence of rampant homosexual practice in and around Rome? Disease as a result of homosexual practice is not new.

A third reason that Paul puts homosexuality first is that he wants to show how much it is against nature. And perhaps he listed Lesbian practice first because woman is God's most glorious creation, and he wanted to show just how low even she could sink if she ignored her conscience. Paul may have hoped to jolt the reader so that he or she might see how their behaviour appeared against the context of God's created order, and be brought to repentance.

I hope that this will happen to many readers, for my ultimate motive in writing this book is to cause one to understand and accept what the Bible says and turn to God. And to cause one to put everything one sees going on in the world into its context, and to see if there is a way out. It may be that you will look back upon reading this as the greatest time of your life, because it turned out to be a life-changing experience.

Now there are four things I want to say about homosexuality in the light of Biblical teaching combined with what I believe to be objective psychological and medical evidence. The first is that homosexuality is abhorrent. It is not ideal. The Bible says it is against nature. Even among animals homosexual practice is something that is almost non-existent. It is exceedingly rare in nature. Moreover, any doctor will tell you that the human body was not made for homosexual intercourse. So the Gay Liberation Movement and the so-called Gay Churches are defying God's created order and plain teaching when they idealise what Scripture and nature regard as an aberration[2].

The second thing is that homosexuality is alien, and not indigenous to nature. God did not make any person homosexual. Sin coming into the world brought about the possibility of aberration. One's environment, parental relationships and other influences allow for homosexuality. As God said in Exodus 34:7, 'Keeping mercy for thousands, forgiving iniquity and transgression and sin, and that I will by no means clear the guilty; visiting the iniquity of the fathers upon the children, and upon the children's children, unto the third and to the fourth generation.' For example, one parent, who mistreats a child, leaves a scar on the child, who grows up, becomes a parent and passes this scar on to the grandchild who in turn becomes a parent. That grandchild passes it on so that the third and fourth generation will feel the scar of sin. So don't ever think that God made anyone a homosexual. It is sin coming into the world which has done it. It is not by God's will.

Something else I have discovered which has been a bit of a surprise to me is that it has become quite speculative to say that one is born a homosexual. Older studies spoke of genetic deficiency or hormone imbalance, but this is now increasingly being disputed. Anthony Store, in his book *Sexual Deviation*, concludes that the homosexual is not born, but made. That one's sexual preference in adult life is determined by the emotional influences to which he was exposed in childhood.

Many years ago a report came out which was considered sensational at the time. The famous Kinsey Report of 1948 (which is now considerably respected by medical people throughout the world) stated that thirty-seven percent of the male population of the United States had a homosexual experience in puberty, but that only four percent of these people were exclusively homosexual if rated on a scale of zero to six. (Zero being exclusively heterosexual, six exclusively homosexual, with bisexuality being in between). That was forty years ago – before the sexual revolution and the rapid disintegration of the family which we have been seeing in recent years. And although the statistics may be dated, they are still looked at by medical people as quite useful and relevant.

It is now believed by many authorities that perhaps one in six males in Britain is homosexual in proclivity. (It is not known how many women are Lesbians. Some say one in ten. Some one in forty-five. In any case it is much rarer). The point is that the so-called invert (six on the Kinsey scale) is quite rare, and many medical and psychological studies are increasingly of the opinion that even the invert does not inherit his behaviour, but acquires it.

This brings me to my third point; homosexuality is acquired and not inherited. This does not mean that the person with homosexual proclivity necessarily chose to be that way, or wants to be that way, for this is a very complex matter, and what I have to say now will obviously be an over-simplification. But there are two perspectives to look at here, and they may overlap psychological causes and precipitating causes.

By psychological causes I mean developmental causes. A book called *The Overt Homosexual* by C. W. Socarides, writing from the psychoanalytic viewpoint, concludes that there is no innate, inborn or genetic factor in homosexuality, but that sexual orientation is 'learned'. It is 'acquired' knowledge and behaviour. This does not mean that this knowledge was consciously or voluntarily acquired. It may go back to childhood, as early as eighteen months of age or before. One man interviewed by a London physician, a so-called invert, said that the earliest memory he had in the world was that of a hand reaching into his crib – and I need not spell out the rest.

Psychoanalytic theory also suggests various psychological causes which are well-known. The weak or absent father, the over-protective mother. The sadistic, punitive, domineering mother. These mainly relate to the male homosexual – but it is generally thought that Lesbianism emerges in the same way. It ought also to be pointed out that Elizabeth Moberly of Cambridge, who is in the psychoanalytic tradition and who writes with a Christian perspective, says that homosexuality is indeed the result of the parent-child relationship being defective. She argues however that the defect lies in the homosexual suffering some deficit in their relationship with the parent of the *same* sex, so that as the child gets older he or she tries to 'make good' that deficit by the medium of the homosexual relationship. (*Homosexuality: a New Christian Ethic*).

Why take time to explore psychological causes? So that all of us would understand that behaviour is caused. But I need not say a lot about all of the precipitating causes. These are immediate causes which promote sexual tension in a homosexual direction. I can give four examples of such situations:

1. *Boarding Schools*. I suppose one could spend a lot of time on this subject. There is ample evidence to show how peer pressure in the public schools breeds homosexual activity, from which some seem never to recover.

2. *Prisons*.

3. *A trauma* may trigger off a fear of the opposite sex. Some believe that at the bottom of all homosexuality is a fear of the opposite sex. There was a relevant story in many of the papers in May 1987, one of which stated, 'President Reagan's adopted son, Michael, has admitted that he was sexually molested and photographed in the nude at the age of seven by a day camp official.' He says, 'For most of my life I worried whether I was a homosexual.' This is but one example of how a trauma may trigger something off with sexual implications.

4. *The rising Feminist Movement*. This phenomenon threatens many men, and often encourages women to be aggressive, which could be called a role reversal. In some cases the Feminist movement is

also encouraging Lesbianism. I now refer to another newspaper article which appeared in 1987, something which is almost so horrifying that I hesitate to quote it. It said, 'Handicapped girl saw Lesbian film. A mentally handicapped girl was shown a video called "How to become a Lesbian in Thirty-five Minutes".' Now I ask, why would anyone want such a thing shown? It demonstrates how that which was once regarded as wicked has been brought out into the open and encouraged.

If you are a homosexual, and you listen to this kind of propaganda which says you should glory in your homosexuality, how can this sort of thing be justified? You know that it is wrong, and it should give you a hint of the satanic influence which is behind it.

My fourth and last point is that homosexuality is avoidable, and not inevitable. Now this may be the hardest point for some to accept, but it is true, and I say it for two reasons. First, at the natural level. Any person who *wants* to change *can* change. Psychologists and doctors – both Christian and non-Christian – have been saying this for years. Second, and most importantly, at the spiritual level. Change is possible through the power of Christ and the care of people who will accept another individual.

The Gay Liberation Movement and the so-called Gay Christian Movement are militating against the idea of changing. Whereas years ago, when a person went to a psychologist or a psychiatrist and uncovered the fact that he was homosexual, the orientation was to change. But today it is rather to accept one's homosexuality and enjoy it. As a result many are no longer motivated to seek help. Obtaining help to change is an uphill climb now.

Thirty years ago people wanted to change but now they are encouraged to accept themselves as homosexual and be proud of it.

But the stories which could be told of what the power of the Gospel can do! My friend Arthur Blessitt told me this story, having returned from California, where he had been at the death bed of a friend who was dying of cancer. The man had been a practising homosexual whom Arthur had led to Christ on Sunset Strip. He was truly converted and God had changed his life. He even got married and had four children. When he was dying he had sent for Arthur and with tears rolling down his cheeks, all he could say was, 'Thank you.'

The Gospel of Jesus Christ is what this book is about. The Gospel – God's word, God is for the homosexual. God does not condemn the homosexual but wants to help him. The same God who says that homosexuality is against nature doesn't just leave you to it.

May I say again that one can change even at the natural level. In 1954 Edward Glover in his book *The Problem of Homosexuality*, based on research at the Portman Clinic, disclosed that out of eighty-one cases studied, thirty-six were cured, twenty-one who had homosexual urges achieved discretion and conscious control, and only seven of the eighty-one were completely unchanged.

The problem today is that because of the sexual revolution homosexuality has been eroticised to such a degree that the practice is encouraged, and many just never imagine having any other lifestyle. The Bible has got it right, and we need to accept that. If Satan is saying to you that you cannot change – that there is no hope, hopefully we have

40

got to you in the nick of time. Perhaps before you contract the HIV virus and develop the fatal disease.

God is against homosexual practice. But he is certainly not against the homosexual.

[1] At the first World Summit on AIDS, held in London during January 1988 (represented by 150 countries), Dr Jonathan Mann, of the World Health Organisation, predicted that, with between five and ten million people already infected with the HIV virus, a million people will be dead or dying from the disease by 1991. He added that this could be an under-estimate.
[2] It is noteworthy that the Chinese Professor Shu-Sheng Wang, addressing the World AIDS Summit Conference in London during January 1988, reported that 'there is no homosexual community as such in China.' He added that Chinese law and 'traditional moral values' prohibit homosexuality. Lest one suppose that the Apostle Paul's view that homosexuality being 'against nature' is only a Christian bias, China could hardly be called a Christian nation.

Chapter Three

Homosexuality and the Christian Faith

AIDS is now regarded as an epidemic throughout the world. In April 1987 *The Times* said that one person a day is now dying of AIDS in Britain[1]. It is also well-known, and beyond controversy, that it is a disease of promiscuity.

I do wish to stress again that there is a difference between homosexual proclivity (preference, orientation) and homosexual practice. It is the latter which the Bible condemns. It is giving in to temptation which is sin, not being tempted.

And I do wish to reaffirm that homosexual practice is no more condemned in the Bible than adultery (heterosexual practice outside of marriage). For we have observed what the Mosiac Law (Leviticus 10) says about the punishment of both homosexuality and adultery. It was death for both. So do not think we have a particular bias against one practice over against another.

We learn from Romans 1:26, 27 that neither homosexual proclivity nor homosexual practice is anything new. Nor is homosexual promiscuity anything new. 'Likewise also the men, leaving the natural use of the woman, burned in their lust one toward another; men with men working that which is unseemly.' Is this a description of your lifestyle? Did you know that it was described in the Bible? It certainly is, and it is put forward as something which is shameful, wrong and against nature. By 'against nature' I do not mean it is not natural to you, but against the way God created mankind – male and female (Gen. 1:27).

We learn also that homosexual plagues are nothing new. Paul says that these men 'received in themselves that particular punishment owing to their perversion,' as the NIV translates the Greek of these words. In the first century hundreds of thousands died from a homosexual disease. Yet the Greek philosophers had intellectualised homosexuality and proclaimed it as the highest bliss. This illustrates another thing we see from Romans 1:26, 27, that emphasis on homosexual primacy – saying that it is the greatest way a person can live – is equally nothing new. But Paul said that they received in themselves the 'due penalty for their perversion'.

It is interesting that women are listed first in verse 26. In the last chapter I suggested three reasons for this. I now suggest yet another reason, because it could be that what is true today was true then. That is that the Lesbians today are actually taking the lead. We not only have the Gay Liberation Movement, but suddenly female homosexuals have come into their own, and have become among the most outspoken members of the movement.

Lesbians are saying some things which are absolutely bizarre. Some Lesbians do not even want to be called woman because 'man' forms part of the word 'woman'. So when they have to write the word they spell it WOMYN or WOMIN. Some are so full of pathological hate that they only want to become pregnant through artificial insemination, and then resent it if they have a boy. They immediately want to have another baby, to have a girl. One Lesbian said that when she had her daughter she was 'complete'. But can you imagine the plight of any poor baby boy being brought up by a mother who holds this kind of concept? A person like this has a deep hurt, and we shouldn't judge them for that hurt. Yet it shows how someone with hostility like that can come to take the lead, and this may have been going on in Paul's day.

We have also been seeing something of the changing picture regarding homosexuality in the last twenty years. What was once regarded as a condition which needed to be changed by medical help, or by counselling, is now regarded as acceptable and even a justifiable alternative lifestyle. It is even condoned by some clergymen. It used to be put forward by psychologists that one can change at the natural level – apart from Christian conversion, that a shift to heterosexual behaviour is a possibility for all homosexuals who are strongly enough motivated to change.

I am asking God, as many read this book to display the power of the Holy Spirit, so that the Gospel can be seen as being what can change your lifestyle. So that when the psychotherapist says to you, 'Just accept yourself – don't try to change – like yourself as you are' – you will know that you can turn to Jesus Christ. God demands repentance, but he supplies the power, and he will not mock you.

These changes in attitude have been brought about largely because of the Sexual Offences Act of 1967 which opened the floodgates to homosexual practice. Now the Gay Liberation Movement not only lobbies for Gay Rights, and resents the idea that homosexuality is treatable, but there are those who want the heterosexual to become like them! All of which is in defiance of Holy Scripture and of God. I say again that studies have increasingly shown that a preference for homosexuality is acquired behaviour, and a majority of men and women who earnestly seek help are actually able to achieve a long-standing reversal of their homosexuality. And I say this stressing that even at the natural level change can happen.

But how much more do those who engage in homosexual practice need to be convinced that what he or she is doing is not only against nature, but that it is also against God's word. For centuries this has been regarded as perversion.

Parallel to all that I have been describing there has come a new development. A man by the name of D. Sherwin Bailey wrote a book called *Homosexuality and the Western Christian Tradition*. He argues that there is no foundation for the prevalent belief that the stories in Genesis 19 and Judges 19 (both of which I have referred to earlier) refer to homosexual sin. This man says that God punished Sodom and Gomorrah for breaching the rules of hospitality, that the men of these cities were simply not being nice to the strangers. He shows a measure of scholarship. He went into the Hebrew word which meant 'to know', and pointed out that this word did not necessarily refer to sexual intercourse.

As a result of these claims a number of New Testament scholars have been forced to examine them. And they have discovered not only sloppy scholarship on the part of D. Sherwin Bailey, but the fact that he was openly bypassing a tradition of Rabbinic Literature which has always seen the incident of Sodom and Gomorrah as sexual sin. This is not to mention Bailey's ignoring 2 Peter 2:6, 8, and Jude 6 – which accuse the men of Sodom of sexual sin, and 'going after strange flesh'.

But what do you suppose has happened? Many among the Gay Christian Movement have adopted Bailey's thesis, despite its having been categorically refuted by competent New Testament Scholarship. And the Gay Christian Youth Movement has also come up with much the same idea. They say that, as for what we have in the Book of Leviticus, that happened before people came into the knowledge of science and psychology that we have now. They explain every one of the verses away and make the claim that the Bible is simply against homosexual promiscuity.

Norman Pittinger, the Cambridge Professor who was known for many years as a theologian of 'process theology', published a book called *Time Before Consent*. In the 1970s many of those who had been homosexuals in private were coming out into the open, and this book became a basis for the justification, among other things, of the so-called Gay Marriage. 'Promiscuity is wrong,' people said, 'but surely there can be a loving relationship between two men or two women.'

One Sunday a man came to see me after an evening service. He said he was a spokesman for the Gay Liberation Movement. He sincerely commended me for my caring but felt that I had misunderstood the point that there can be such a thing as a real loving relationship between homosexuals. He too was against promiscuity. But was there not such a thing as two men or two women being in committed love?

How does one answer that? In the same way as one replies to those who have committed adultery. I have had much experience in the vestry of people coming in and describing a certain situation to me. And it goes like this nearly every time. 'I know that what I am doing would generally be thought of as being wrong – but I am in love with this woman and she's in love with me. I know she's married, and I'm married, but you just don't understand the love we feel. This is real – it has got to be all right.' They all claim that they are the one exception. And it is often the same with homosexual practice.

Why is homosexual practice sin? I will give three reasons. The first – which I have already dealt with – is that it defies the natural order. In Genesis 1 verse 27 we read, 'So God created man in his own image, in the image of God created he him; male and female created he them.' And God said, 'It is not good that man should be alone; I will make him an help meet for him' (Ch. 2:18). When God created Eve the sexes were differentiated. And marriage was instituted, with its relational and conceptional purpose. Relational to bring mutual fulfilment; it was God's answer to the problem of loneliness. Conceptional to populate the earth. So homosexual practice is sin because it defies this natural order.

The second reason is that it goes against the New Testament understanding of love. In the ancient Greek language there were three words which translated into English as the word 'love'. One is *philia* from which the city of Philadelphia is named, 'the City of Brotherly Love'. It was brotherly love, family love. The love of a mother for a child or a brother for a sister. Then there was *eros*. Erotic, or

47

physical love. And that is the kind of love which is talked about so much today. But people forget that *eros* love is insufficient to bring about commitment and fulfilment. For the truth is that *eros* love does not last. This is why marriages break down. And it is why homosexual commitments form the most inconsistent pattern in the world. *Eros* love does not last. Why else would a famous movie star, married seven times be looking now for her eighth husband? For this kind of love – that makes a man and a woman want to get married, although it is natural and God-given is *not* the love that will sustain that marriage. Another love must emerge, and if it doesn't, that marriage is likely to be shattered in a matter of time.

So what is this third type of love? It is from the Greek word, *agape*, which is almost always used in the New Testament to describe an unselfish love. The verb form of *agape* is used this way in John 3:16, 'For God so *loved* the world, that he *gave* his only begotten Son, that whosoever believeth in him *should not perish*, but have everlasting life'. This is the love which is described in 1 Corinthians 13, the 'love chapter' of the Bible. It is the love by which the Christian is to live his life, so that if a person walks in this love he will fulfil the Law.

Any person walking in *agape* love will neither commit adultery nor homosexuality. It is impossible to walk in it and commit such sin. This is why Paul could say, 'Owe no man any thing, but to love one another; for he that loveth another hath fulfilled the law. For this, Thou shalt not commit adultery, Thou shalt not kill, Thou shalt not steal, Thou shalt not bear false witness, Thou shalt not covet; and if there be any other commandment, it is briefly comprehended in this saying, namely, Thou shalt love thy neighbour as thyself. Love worketh no ill to his neighbour: therefore love is the fulfilling of the law' (Rom. 13:8–10). Moreover, *agape* love will never leave a person with a feeling of guilt! But any sexual practice outside of marriage will leave you feeling guilty. Marriage alone is sanctioned by God. And only sexual union within marriage leaves a person without any guilt feelings. 'Marriage is honourable in all, and the bed undefiled' (Heb. 13:4). Heterosexual adultery or homosexual practice – even where the latter is described as a so-called committed relationship – are based on *eros* love and not *agape*. And they will always leave you feeling guilty and will *end badly*.

If you are thinking of entering into an affair – whether it is premarital sex, adultery, or homosexual activity and you can see the opportunity looming, let me make you a faithful prediction: *it will end badly*. It may start out making you feel excited and you may think, 'Ah, this is wonderful.' But it will end badly.

The third reason why homosexual practice is sin is that it never gives lasting peace or fulfilment. And this is typical of sin. There is an interesting thing about the sin which is described in Genesis 19. Sodom was an obviously wicked city. It had been described as wicked before God ever rained fire and brimstone on it (Gen. 13:13). But when Lot had the two visitors, whom the Bible says were angels, the men of Sodom and gomorrah were aroused. Why? Because they had to have something *different*. Because this kind of sexual fulfilment just doesn't fulfil. It always wants something different. In my research of this subject I have come across practices that I had never dreamed of – that I never knew

49

existed. Shameful things which I could not repeat in this book. This lifestyle always breeds the desire for something new and different. One psychiatrist I interviewed told me that it is estimated that many homosexuals in the city of San Francisco will have twenty-five thousand partners in a lifetime. And some have to have five or six partners a day. It is not, therefore, surprising that one person in fifteen has AIDS in that city, where over a third – some now say it is one half – of the population are homosexual.

We are living in a day in which not only homosexuality but also heterosexual promiscuity are eroticised and this leaves the impression that such is something you *must* do. You can't escape – you must have fulfilment! Sex magazines glamorise adultery and premarital sex. Yet this is interesting, fresh Government statistics came out last year showing the declining marriage situation, and how more divorces are taking place than ever. But do you know what they found out about those who had slept together before they were married – those who had tried it out? The ratio of divorce among that group was the *same as for everyone else*. So the idea that you need to try each other out for a while doesn't work. These marriages were ending in divorce as well.

One of the biggest myths of all is that the homosexual has a greater sex drive. The Wolfenden Report (which was the very thing which led to the Sexual Offences Act) even points this out. Yet it is something that not many people realise. The homosexual does *not* have any greater sexual need than anybody else. All the psychiatric studies confirm this. But in this age of the so-called Metropolitan Churches – the Gay Christian Churches – people will not accept this.

It is not sex but marriage which is the God-ordained analogy in relation to his people. Christ loved the Church. Christ the bridegroom loved the Church, which is the Bride. So that marriage is four things: *committed*, *exclusive*, *heterosexual* and *permanent*. That is what the Bible says about marriage.

Why then should you or anybody else make the decision to come to Christ? Answer: because the blood that Jesus shed on the cross will take all guilt away. You may say you don't feel guilty, and you can go on kidding yourself. But I know better, and so do you. Would you not just like to feel *clean* inside? I can tell you that you can. Jesus of Nazareth, the Son of God, suffered a shameful death on a cross but the blood that he shed satisfied God's justice – and that blood can cleanse today. You can lose all of your guilty stains, for the fountain filled with Christ's blood will wash them all away. It can't change the past. It may not change your sexual tendency. But it can break the power of sin. So that you can do one of two things. Be celibate, live without, as many heterosexuals do. Or come to Christ and watch him change you. He has done it thousands of times.

The Holy Spirit can change your lifestyle. Paul said when he wrote to the Church at Corinth, 'Be not deceived; neither fornicators, nor idolaters, nor adulterers, nor effeminate' (that's the Authorised Version's way of translating 'the homosexual') nor abusers of themselves with mankind . . . shall inherit the kingdom of God'. But he goes on, 'And such *were some of you*; but yet are washed, but ye are sanctified, but ye are justified in the name of the Lord Jesus' (1 Cor. 6:9–12). So there were those in the Church at Corinth who had been homosexuals. But they were washed. And this is what the Gospel can do.

Let me give you another reason for coming to Christ. Think about the consequences of sin; here on earth there is guilt, sorrow, despair – not to mention the fear of disease. You will live in perpetual fear. Because something has happened in the last decade which has changed everything, and maybe your lifestyle is going to have to change anyway. Consider the consequences of sin – all that you will suffer here below. But that is not all. Jesus said, 'And if thy hand offend thee, cut it off: it is better for thee to enter into life maimed, than having two hands to go into hell, into the fire that never shall be quenched. Where their worm dieth not, and the fire is not quenched. And if thy foot offend thee, cut it off: it is better for thee to enter halt into life, than having two feet to be cast into hell, into the fire that never shall be quenched; where their worm dieth not, and the fire is not quenched. And if thine eye offend thee, pluck it out; it is better for thee to enter into the kingdom of God with one eye, than having two eyes to be cast into hell fire' (Mark 9:43–47).

Maybe you have not heard that before, and if you have not, then the modern Church has failed you in not warning you of the wrath of God to come. You were made for God. As Saint Augustine put it, 'Thou hast made us for thyself; our souls are restless until they find their rest in thee.' And you are not an animal. When you die eternity begins, and it lasts a long time – for ever and ever and ever. Listen to the words of John Newton about those who are saved:

'When we've been there ten thousand years, bright shining as the Sun.
We've no less days to sing God's praise than when we first begun.'

And the reverse is true. After ten thousand years in hell it is as though it had just begun. So think about the consequences of sin.

C. S. Lewis made four interesting observations in a letter before he died. First, that physical satisfaction of homosexual desire is sin. Secondly, that leaves the homosexual no worse off than any heterosexual person who is prevented for whatever reason from marrying. Thirdly, that the homosexual has to accept sexual abstinence just as the poor man has to forego certain pleasures because he cannot afford them. And finally, any homosexual who accepts his cross and puts himself under divine guidance will be shown the way.

I also want to say that I do sympathise with a loneliness which I suspect I myself have never known. Anthony Store, in his book *Sexual Deviation*, makes this comment, 'The average man who has a wife to come home to has little idea of the depth of loneliness to which the homosexual can sink, or of the strength of the compulsive urge for sexual contact which drives him.'

But Jesus knows. And I believe you will find in God's providence a caring Church which will not judge you or make fun of you.

And if you want to come to Christ he will forgive you. It may mean a life of abstinence, without ever being married. I don't know, but you must be willing for that. Jesus understands. He 'was in all points tempted like as we are, yet without sin' (Heb. 4:15). I call on you right now to confess Christ openly.

---

[1]According to *The Times* (12th January 1988) at least five people every day are becoming infected with the HIV virus.

Chapter Four

Jesus and AIDS

It began suddenly in the Autumn of 1979. Young homosexual men with a history of promiscuity started showing up at the medical clinics in New York City, Los Angeles, San Francisco, with a bizarre array of ailments. Some had a strange kind of pneumonia – a deadly disease rarely seen except in drug-weakened cancer and transplant patients. Others bore the purplish skin lesions of Kaposi's sarcoma, a cancer which is usually confined to elderly men of Mediterranean extraction or young men in Equatorial Africa. The doctors didn't know what to make of this strange phenomenon, but all these men had one thing in common – an immune system so severely weakened that they were living playgrounds for infectious agents. As soon as one bug could be brought under control these patients would fall prey to another. They gradually wasted away. They all died. But new people kept showing up with the same disease (from *Time* magazine's first AIDS story, 6th September, 1982).

Sixteen months later, in 1981, the Centre of Disease Control in Atlanta, Georgia, decided what it was, and came up with a carefully thought out name. They used an acrostic because they wanted to capture the imagination of the world. For it would appear that what had hit the world was in the early stages of a plague which could prove more severe than anything known in the history of the human race. They called it AIDS – Acquired Immune Deficiency Syndrome – the resulting condition of a virus infection which destroys the body's defence mechanism against infection.

And since 1981 the HIV virus, which is the start of AIDS, has been isolated in no fewer than seventy-seven countries. In some parts of Africa one fifth of the sexually active population are infected. In some cities in America the majority of male homosexuals are already infected. In all countries both the HIV virus and AIDS are more common in cities than in rural areas. The virus is found in semen, vaginal fluid, blood, saliva, breast milk, urine and tears, but the main spread is by sexual intercourse, and over seventy-five percent of victims are male homosexuals. Once infected, a person remains infected for the rest of his life. And those who are infected are also infectious. That is, they are carriers of the virus, and can transmit it to others by means of sexual intercourse or by their blood. (The question of whether the virus can spread by kissing is still open. Most people say it cannot, but Dr Ruth Jarrett of Glasgow University has pointed out that there is one well documented case of someone catching AIDS through heavy kissing). Once infected with the HIV virus, the person remains at risk of getting AIDS for years – perhaps the rest of his life.

Let me give you an idea of how quickly this thing is spreading. In America the estimated number of people infected with the HIV virus in September 1981 was twelve thousand. In July 1982 it was fifty one thousand; in January 1983, one hundred and two thousand; in April 1984 four hundred and eleven thousand. In February 1985 eight hundred and twenty two thousand; in January 1986 one million, six hundred and forty five thousand and in January 1987, the figure was two million nine hundred thousand. In New York, AIDS is now the most common cause of death in *women* aged 25–34.

It is not known how many of those with the HIV virus will contract AIDS. At present at least twenty percent of them contract it. But with the present state of medical knowledge, those who have the virus will always have it and may always be susceptible to developing AIDS. I have talked with a number of medical people who privately believe that *all* who have the HIV virus will contract AIDS eventually. It is too early to know this for sure. What is known is that one with the HIV virus, who at present does not have AIDS will none the less be able to pass the virus to another who will get AIDS. The estimated time of incubation is up to nine years, although some say up to fifteen years. No cure has been found, nor is there an effective vaccine. At present all who get AIDS die. Dr Patrick Dixon in his book *The Truth About AIDS* has put it like this. 'The numbers already doomed in the USA make Vietnam look like a children's playground. The coffins, if placed end to end, would stretch for 1,000 miles.' But there is prevention – and that is either celibacy or heterosexual monogamy. In other words, one partner in the bond of marriage.

But what is happening in Britain? As we said, *The Times* in April 1987 reported that one person a day is now dying from AIDS in Britain.

So I must raise the question – is AIDS the judgement

of God? John Lubbock, the nineteenth century English astronomer and mathematician, said, 'Our duty is to believe that for which we have sufficient evidence, and to suspend our judgement when we have not.' So our task is to answer the question, 'Is there sufficient evidence to believe that the deadly spread of AIDS, is in some sense the judgement of God?' Now this question naturally arises because of the association of AIDS with homosexual promiscuity generally, and the Biblical response to homosexual practice particularly. Such a question does not appear to come up very often with reference to other illnesses such as heart disease, lung cancer, alcoholism or even drug addiction.

Did many think of the question of judgement when the sudden 'flu epidemics broke out a few years ago? For all I know, this question may have been relevant to all those as well. But since at the moment over seventy-five percent of AIDS victims are homosexual, and since the HIV virus has reached the heterosexual community through bisexual contact or promiscuity, it is natural to ask, 'Is AIDS the judgement of God?'

Three facts will not be disputed. With very few exceptions:

1. AIDS is a disease of promiscuity, and it is spreading rapidly.

2. At the present time all AIDS victims die, because no cure has been found.

3. The only absolute prevention is, as I have said, either celibacy or heterosexual monogamy.

I want to raise three cautions here which must govern our approach to this serious and complex subject. Because I have wanted urgently to know the truth, so I governed myself by these, which I now hope will guide all of us. Firstly, we must avoid a gut reaction to the question. And there are two extremes such a reaction may take. One is the opinion of the Metropolitan Community Church, which speaks for the so-called Gay Christian Movement. They say AIDS is not a judgement, if only because lesbians do not appear to be affected by it[1]. The other extreme is to share the opinion of certain evangelicals, who want the answer to be yes. Now I think some evangelicals are aching to see God work. If not through signs and wonders, then through judgement. They may want a signs and wonders syndrome in reverse! One minister, alas, has actually said he hoped they never find a cure for AIDS. In between these extremes you have the view that AIDS is simply the consequence of sin.

The second caution is that we must be cleansed from the idea that homosexual promiscuity is singularly cursed by God. Now Romans 1:26, 27 does describe homosexual promiscuity as being a sign that God had given such people over to vile affections, 'For this cause God gave them up unto vile affections, for even their women did change the natural use into that which is against nature, and likewise also the men, leaving the natural use of the woman, burned in their lust one toward another; men with men working that which is unseemly, and receiving in themselves that recompense of their error which was meet.' But Romans 1:28, 29 equally describe *heterosexual* promiscuity as being evidence of a 'reprobate mind' (v28). So both types of promiscuity are condemned. And yet such reprobation is further depicted in that God had given some up to covetousness, envying and gossiping (v29).

Homosexual practice is called an abomination in

Leviticus 18:22. Leviticus 20:3 calls for the homosexual to be put to death, but verse 10 of the same chapter calls for both the adulterer and the adulteress to be put to death also. And Proverbs 6:16–19 lists as abominations 'a proud look, a lying tongue, and hands that shed innocent blood, an heart that deviseth wicked imaginations, feet that be swift in running to mischief, a false witness that speaketh lies, and he that soweth discord between brethren.' So let no one think that the homosexual is being singled out by God or that homosexuality is a worse sin. Furthermore, homosexuals and adulterers are in the group of those in Corinth who had been converted to Jesus Christ (1 Corinthians 6:9–11).

The third caution which must govern our approach is something which I have stated above but which I want to emphasise again – we must be cleansed of homophobia; an irrational fear or hatred of, or even a revulsion toward the homosexual. Many people treat homosexuals in the way people treated lepers in Jesus' day. But how did Jesus treat lepers? He accepted them and he cleansed them. We are told that Jesus was 'in all points tempted like as we are, yet without sin.' So that he is 'touched with the feeling of our infirmities' (Heb. 4:15).

Whatever one's particular problem is – it may not be sexual – it may be greed or envy, or you may be eaten up with anger and wanting vengeance; Jesus understands your problem even if no one else does. And Jesus doesn't moralise. He doesn't make you feel awful or wicked and dirty. He is 'touched with the feeling of our weaknesses' and he went all the way to the cross and shed his blood for our sins. Jesus didn't die for his own sins, because he never sinned (2 Cor. 5:21). He was free from sin in thought, word and deed. He died for *our* sins. Isaiah the prophet said, 'The Lord hath laid on him the iniquity of us all' (Is. 53:6).

It is only to the degree that we want to be like Jesus that we will get God's opinion on this question, Is AIDS the judgement of God? We must be aware of certain scriptures. The apostle Paul said of God 'How unsearchable are his judgements, and his ways past finding out!' (Rom. 11:33). Isaiah said, 'For my thoughts are not your thoughts, neither are your ways my ways, saith the Lord. For as the heavens are higher than the earth, so are my ways higher than your ways, and my thoughts than your thoughts' (Is. 55:8, 9). Jesus said once to the Pharisees and all who listened, 'Ye can discern the face of the sky; but can ye not discern the signs of the times?' (Matt. 16:3).

It is a very sobering thought that if God is sending a signal to our generation, then the judgement is surely upon us if we miss it. For the worst judgement of all is not AIDS, but a failure to hear the word of the Lord in the land (Amos 8:11). According to John Calvin, part of the message of the prophet Joel was the reproving of the stupidity of the people for not seeing the invasion of locusts as God's judgement. God therefore threatened the people with more grievous evils if they did not repent.

So if we are witnessing certain tokens of God's displeasure, we may mark it down that if the judgement sent upon us does not result in some change, then things will get worse. So what we are dealing with is grave indeed. If AIDS is the judgement of God and we don't see it that way and don't change our ways, it will get worse. And yet if we are witnessing tokens of God's displeasure we should not expect everyone to see it at first. Jeremiah stood alone for a number of years in forecasting the Babylonian captivity.

But what did Jesus have to say with regard to the subject of God sending judgement? This surely is the place at which we must begin. In my own research, and in my own attempts to get an answer, I have sincerely wanted to be like Jesus. So I begin with what Jesus' opinion was on the subject of judgement.

Now maybe the very *idea* of God sending judgement is repulsive to some. Maybe it smacks of a God you don't want to have anything to do with anyway. Or perhaps you are one of those who says, 'Well, I do like Jesus. I can accept him, but I can't accept a God who sends judgement.' Are you like that? Then let's listen to Jesus.

The first thing that we need to know about Jesus in this connection is that he never apologised for the God of the Bible, and the God of the Old Testament is the God who sends judgement and who punishes sin. And the fact is that not only did Jesus *not* apologise for the God of the Old Testament, he had more to say about God's wrath and punishment than anyone else in the New Testament.

But Jesus never singled out an individual except for the implicit threat of damnation for not eventually believing the promise. Jesus said (in John 3:16, which Martin Luther called the Bible in a nutshell) 'For God so loved the world, that he gave his only begotten Son, that whosoever believeth in him should not perish, but have everlasting life.' So according to Jesus any individual who doesn't believe the Gospel (that is, the good news that he came to die on a cross for our sin) will perish. To that extent Jesus pronounced judgement on an individual, but only within the context of the general promise and warning. He never singled out one person and said, 'God is getting at you.'

There are two New Testament passages that will bear our examination. First, in Luke 13:1–5. There were those present who told Jesus about certain Galileans whose blood Pilate had mixed with their sacrifices. Jesus tried to figure out what they were getting at in telling him this, and he just said to them, 'Do you think that those Galileans were worse sinners than all the other Galileans because they suffered in this way?'

Now the equivalent of that today is this. There are those who – if I may put it this way – are unlucky enough to contract AIDS. But are they worse sinners? Jesus' answer is 'No.' But Jesus went on to say to those who thought they were so righteous, 'Except ye repent, ye shall all likewise perish.' Jesus continued, as it were, 'While we are talking, let me remind you of those eighteen who died when the Tower of Siloam fell on them – Do you think they were more guilty than all the others living in Jerusalem? No. But unless you repent you too will perish.'

The second passage that is very relevant here is John 9:1–3. We are told that Jesus saw a man who was blind from birth. His disciples said, 'Master, who did sin, this man or his parents, that he was born blind?' And Jesus answered, 'Neither hath this man sinned, nor his parents. But this happened that the works of God should be made manifest in him.' And he went on to heal the man!

It is possible therefore that a person could be healed of AIDS. I look forward to seeing if God is going to do this in our day. For such would show God wonderfully at work in our generation. So many miracles are alleged to take place nowadays, but when you get to the bottom to find out if they really do happen, there is so often a doubt, or some natural explanation. But if someone were healed of AIDS it would be a sign of God's power and mercy indeed. And we should pray for that, and hope for it.

These two passages rule out the idea that anybody who has AIDS is singularly cursed of God. So whether it be the thirty babies in the United Kingdom who have the HIV virus at the moment; or the hundreds of babies in West Germany who reportedly have the HIV virus; or that first baby to die who caught AIDS through a blood transfusion; or even those who through sexual promiscuity were unlucky in catching AIDS, can you say that any of these were singularly cursed of God?

'No,' according to Jesus. For according to him even those who are celibate – whether homosexual or heterosexual – even those who are shining examples of marital fidelity, will eventually perish under God's judgement if they don't repent. There may be someone reading this book who thinks, 'Well, I'm innocent of all this.' Perhaps you have a revulsion for homosexuality and you hope God is against the homosexual. Listen, reader, if you don't repent of your self-righteousness you too will perish! And God will allow you to go to hell just as quickly as an immoral person who may have a background of damaged emotions that you have not been exposed to. Never think that one person is the example of God's judgement. Because the judgement of God, according to Jesus, is ultimately carried out indiscriminately upon *all* who do not confess him as Lord and Saviour.

However, Jesus did not hesitate to pronounce judgement upon a *community*. On an individual, no. On a community of people, yes. In Matthew 10, he said to those disciples who he had sent out, 'And whosoever shall not receive you, nor hear your words, when ye depart out of that house or city, shake off the dust of your feet. Verily I say unto you, it shall be more tolerable for the land of Sodom and Gomorrah the day of judgement, than for that city (vv. 14, 15). In Matthew 11, Jesus said 'Woe unto thee, chorazin! Woe unto thee, Bethsaida! . . . And thou, Capernaum, which are exalted unto heaven, shalt be brought down to hell . . . I say unto you, that it shall be more tolerable for the land of Sodom in the day of judgement, than for thee' (vv 23, 24). In Matthew 23 Jesus categorically condemned scribes and pharisees, calling them hypocrites and serpents, saying, 'How can ye escape the damnation of hell?' (v 33).

But he condemned them as a group, not as individuals. Again in Matthew 23 he said that judgement would come upon his generation, and concluded 'O Jerusalem, Jerusalem, thou that killest the prophets and stonest them which are sent unto thee, how often would I have gathered thy children together, even as a hen gathereth her chickens under her wings and ye would not! Behold, your house is left unto you desolate' (v 37, 38). And so Jesus could pronounce judgement upon a group, a city or a generation (and he did so with tears). But never on an individual.

Jesus' attitude toward any repentant sinner is, 'Neither do I condemn thee – go, and sin no more' (John 8:11). So whoever you are, if you have fallen into sin – sexual sin, any kind of sin – you may feel that the world is against you, and that society condemns you. But Jesus is not against you. His word to you is, 'I don't condemn you. Go and sin no more'.

But never think that Jesus' withholding judgement upon an individual gives one licence to continue. No. Jesus said to the woman who was found in the act of adultery, 'Go and sin no more.' And so this must be the Christian attitude towards the promiscuous homosexual with AIDS, or the promiscuous hetero-sexual with AIDS, who has the same opportunity to be saved as the dying thief on the cross whom Jesus forgave (Luke 23:39–43).

But I now answer the question 'Is AIDS God's Judgment?' Yes. Because AIDS is essentially a disease of promiscuity. It is God's judgement, yes, but not upon a single person. It is a judgement upon promiscuity. I came to this conclusion partly by asking the questions, Why is all of this taking place now? Why not a hundred years ago? Why not fifty years ago? According to Romans Chapter 1 sexual promiscuity is nothing new.

The first evidence of AIDS came to light in the Autumn of 1979. But it is thought that the virus was present in the 'swinging sixties' – the same era which paralleled the full blown culmination of neo-orthodoxy and liberalism in the Church. It paralleled the arrival of 'situation ethics', the idea was that there are no absolute moral standards; that there are exceptions, such as adultery being all right in certain cases. Now in more recent years some are advocating homosexual marriage.

I suspect that during the sixties God looked down on the world he loves and decided to do something in order to let the world see that he is a Holy God. That he cares. That he hates sin, and that we are made in the image of God and have been bought with a price (1 Cor. 6:20). Who would have thought the day would come when men are seriously saying that it may be safer to 'make war, not love'? F. W. Faber wrote the hymn which includes this remarkable verse:

'There's a wideness in God's mercy,
Like the wideness of the Sea.
There's a kindness in his justice,
Which is more than liberty.'

These words were written by F. W. Faber who, according to Geoffrey Faber in his book *Oxford Apostles*, was a non-practising homosexual and could write those words 'There's a kindness in his justice, which is more than liberty'.

All of us ought to know, whatever our own sexual proclivity, that the Bible got it right. For if I decide to defy God's way I will pay for it. I urge you, if you are engaged in any kind of sexual activity that is not within the bonds of marriage, stop it. If you are engaged in premarital sex, stop it. If you are engaged in homosexual practice, stop it. If you are having an extra-marital affair – in the name of God, stop it.

Remember these words, 'Be sure your sin will find you out' (Numb. 32:23). You need to know that whatever your sin is, you will be exposed. It is only a matter of time.

Those who get AIDS die sooner. But we are all going to die. Are you ready to die? Maybe your sin is gossiping, maybe it is lying. Or stealing. Or hate. Or I dare say that you are so moral and upright that your self-righteousness is vile in God's sight? Jesus was actually more sympathetic towards a person with a sexual sin than he was towards self-righteousness.

[1] *The AIDS Letter*, produced by the Royal Society of Medicine (Volume 1, Number 4, December 1987), refers to two documented cases of female-to-female HIV transmissions.

Chapter Five

AIDS: What Kind of Judgement?

'In this country there is hysteria over the non-sexual risks of catching AIDS and total apathy about the sexual risks, which are much greater.'

Dr Patrick Dixon, author of
The Truth About AIDS

It has been called the Gay Plague. It has been called the plague of the century. It is regarded by many authorities as possibly the most devastating thing to hit mankind in the history of the human race. AIDS: in what sense is it God's judgement?

We saw in the previous chapter how Jesus looked on this kind of thing. Jesus never pronounced judgement on one person. He never said, 'You are being judged by God because this has happened to you.' Instead, what he said was that the most moral person in the world needs to repent before God just as much as the most wicked person who ever lived. For the person who is 'wicked' has only been allowed to explore that is in the hearts of all men. The truth is that self-righteousness is, if anything, more awful in the sight of God than the worst form of immorality.

Jesus in any case never pronounced judgement on a single individual. What he said was, 'Neither do I

condemn thee: go, and sin no more' (John 8:11).
But he pronounced judgement upon communities of
people. He thus judged Jerusalem. And he could
judge a whole generation. But his attitude towards
the sinner was, 'Neither do I condemn thee: go, and
sin no more.'

This must be the Christian attitude towards the
promiscuous homosexual or heterosexual who is
unlucky enough to get AIDS. For when Jesus was on
the cross he was between two other crosses. On one
side was the thief who said, 'Lord, remember me
when thou comest into thy kingdom.' And Jesus
turned to him and said, 'Today shalt thou be with
me in paradise' (Luke 23:42, 43). Here was a person
converted minutes before he died. And this is the
marvel of the grace of God.

Of course this is the very thing a lot of people
don't like about the grace of God. They say, 'Are
you telling me that a person can live an immoral life
right to the end and suddenly be saved? And someone else can live a good life – not give in to
immorality – and go to hell?' Yes. We need to know
that anybody who is saved is saved entirely by the
grace of God, so that we can never boast (Ephesians
2:8, 9).

Is AIDS God's judgement? Yes. But that 'yes'
isn't the end of the story. For in the Bible there are
no fewer than *five* categories of judgement. We also
need to know that there is nowhere else to look for
the answer to our question but in the Bible. For all
that I am saying is to be found there. So if AIDS is
the judgement of God, what kind of judgement is it?
And here there is no easy answer to the question.

In this chapter I will explain five types of
judgement. I will list them now and explain each of

them below. They are: (1) retributive judgement,
(2) gracious judgement, (3) redemptive judgement,
(4) natural judgement and (5) silent judgement.
The first four of these five categories clearly emerge
in the third chapter of Genesis, where there is given
the account of how Adam and Eve, our first parents,
sinned in the Garden of Eden.

What is retributive judgement? It is when God
gets even. When his anger is poured out. God said to
Adam, 'Of every tree of the garden thou mayest
freely eat: But of the tree of knowledge of good and
evil, thou shalt not eat of it: for in the say that thou
eatest thereof thou shalt surely die' (Gen. 2:16, 17).
The Hebrew actually reads, 'Dying thou shalt die.'
So Romans 6:23 could say, 'The wages of sin is
death.' What do you get for sinning? Death. 'All
have sinned' (Romans 3:23). All must die. Retributive judgement is God getting even and showing
no mercy at all.

Gracious judgement, on the other hand, is *partly*
retributive and *partly* merciful – but it is *always* a
warning. Whilst retributive judgement is 'the wrath
of God without mixture' (Rev. 14:10), gracious
judgement is mixed with mercy. Jesus said, 'As
many as I love, I rebuke and chasten' (Rev. 3:19).
Therefore where there is gracious judgement,
painful though it is, there is also hope. This type of
judgement *can* therefore be partly retributive – to the
point of plagues coming. But why? In order to
induce repentance. When he is angry God may send
judgement, yes. But he is doing it to warn us, to stop
us. He may send a plague in order to turn us
around.

This is what happened with Jonah. God said to
Jonah, 'Arise, go to Nineveh, that great city, and

cry against it; for their wickedness is come up before me' (Jonah 1:2). But Jonah said, 'No, I can't do that,' and he ran from God. (Are you running from God?) So God sent a great fish and it swallowed up Jonah. It was judgement but it was mostly a warning. Gracious judgement. For the fish ejected Jonah on dry land. God came to Jonah the second time and said, 'Go,' and Jonah went. Therefore what was at the bottom of everything was gracious judgement.

The third kind of judgement – redemptive judgement – is partly retribution and partly *promise*. This can be seen on an occasion when the Children of Israel murmured against God. (Now do you know that God doesn't like murmuring at all? You may feel bitter, or angry – you may want to shake your fist at God. But be very careful. Your murmuring always seems justified at the time, but you need to know that God doesn't like it.) When the Children of Israel murmured God sent poisonous snakes which bit the people. People were dying all over the place. But then God said to Moses, 'Make thee a fiery serpent, and set it upon a pole: and it shall come to pass, that every one that is bitten, when he looketh upon it, shall live' (Numb. 21:8). And Moses held up the serpent of brass and all those who looked at it lived. So what was at the bottom line here was redemptive judgement. This is a variation of gracious judgement. God sent a warning, but with an explicit promise; that those who would 'look' at the serpent would live.

I call the fourth category – natural judgement. This is a variation of retributive judgement with the emphasis being on the inevitable consequences of sin. It is a principle which may be summed up in the phrase, 'You reap what you sow.' There is a natural judgement at work. And many people believe that the AIDS phenomenon is to be best explained simply as the consequence of sin. That it is a natural law at work. There is a lot to be said for this. I will return to it below.

The final category is silent judgement – when God appears to do nothing. This to me is the scariest judgement of all. If I have learned anything from a careful study of Romans 1 it is that when God is 'angriest' he does *nothing*. God never loses his temper like you and I do. We may think that if God gets really mad he's just going to show it right now! But God isn't like that. 'The wrath of man worketh not the righteousness of God' (Jas. 1:20). We may think we can tempt God. We may think we can needle him, or challenge him to send a bolt of lightning! But the angrier God is, the calmer he is. Because time is on his side. He can wait. He has an awful lot of patience.

In a word; when God is at his angriest he doesn't do anything. He doesn't send pain. He doesn't even send a warning. When sin and promiscuity prosper, when those who have defied God go right on and you say, 'Dear Lord, how can you let people do that?' remember that the Psalmist also raised this question. In Psalm 37 he said, 'Fret not thyself because of him who prospereth in his way . . . (v 1). 'For they shall soon be cut down like the grass' (v 2). Even if that 'soon' can seem to us like an eternity and we wonder why God doesn't do something. Twenty years ago a minister in the United States said that if God doesn't judge America he should raise up Sodom and Gomorrah and apologise to them.

When sin goes on unabated it suggests silent judgement. But do you know what this means? If you are able to get away with something that, according to the Bible is wrong, but God does nothing, it suggests that he is *not* going to deal with your sin *now*. But you are going to have to stand before God some day and give an account of all that you did. And it is *then* that God's undiluted, retributive judgement will be meted out. And the consequences of sin in eternity are such that no human orator, preacher or logician can begin to explain or to describe how awful God's wrath is!

These categories already show the complex nature of our subject. That is not all; more than one category can be in operation simultaneously, and usually is. For example, death came into the world as a consequence of sin. That was retributive judgement. But redemption was also offered.

Indeed, four of these categories of judgement emerge in the book of Genesis. (1) Retributive judgement. 'In the day that thou eatest thereof thou shalt surely die' (Ch. 2:17). (2) Gracious judgement. 'And they heard the voice of the Lord God walking in the garden in the cool of the day . . . And the Lord God called unto Adam, and said unto him, "Where art thou?" ' (Ch. 3:8, 9). It was gracious of God to do this. He could have executed a total silence. (3) Redemptive judgement. This was wonderfully in operation immediately after man's fall when came the first promise of the Redeemer in the Bible: 'And I will put enmity between thee and the woman, and between thy seed and her seed; it shall bruise thy head, and thou shalt bruise his heel' (Gen. 3:15). And in Genesis 3:21 we read, 'Unto Adam also and to his wife did the Lord God make coats of skins, and clothed them,' which implies the sacrifice of blood; thus redemption was in operation. (4) Natural judgement. Clearly seen is the consequence of sin. Adam and Eve 'knew that they were naked; and they sewed fig leaves together, and made themselves aprons' (Ch. 3:7). One of the consequences of sin is guilt and shame and an effort to hide that guilt.

Are you reading these lines and know that what you are doing is wrong? And I am not just addressing sexual immorality. There are many who are playing fast and loose with their own lives in other ways. You know what you have been up to is wicked but do you think you can get away with it? But why, then, do you hide it and attempt to justify it? Remember that in Genesis, although Adam and Eve clothed themselves, they felt awful. They were afraid and hid themselves.

Now these judgements all have their subsidiary, parallel and permanent consequences. For example, a part of the result of the sin of Adam and Eve was (1) the pain of child bearing (Gen. 3:16); (2) the ground being cursed (v 17) and (3) man working by the sweat of his brow (v 19).

In Genesis 4, although God was unhappy with Cain's offering, he gave Cain a second chance – which was gracious judgement. But Cain stuck to his guns, then killed Abel his brother and God's retributive judgement followed. Cain said, 'My punishment is greater than I can bear (Gen. 4:13). That is typical of retributive judgement. There is no mixture of mercy or hope. Should it come to you or me, we won't be able to bear it.

In Noah's day God saw that 'the wickedness of man was great in the earth, and that every imagination of the thoughts of his heart was only evil continually' (Gen. 6:5). In Genesis 6:3 we read that God said, 'My spirit shall not always strive with man.' Retributive judgement followed, and the world was destroyed by the flood. But in all this there was redemptive mercy for Noah's family.

In my preparation one of the things I often do when I have to deal with a new word is to see how the word is used in the Bible the first time. I have been sometimes intrigued by what is called 'the law of first mention', the idea that a word carries a special meaning right through Scripture as it had when it first appeared. It is sometimes worthwhile. I looked up the word 'plague' to see when it first appeared in the Bible. It is in Genesis 12:17. Abraham had lied about Sarah – he said she was his sister, and when she was taken into Pharaoh's house God sent 'plagues'. But these plagues were stayed, which shows they were a sign of *gracious* judgement – to both Pharaoh and Abraham. It also shows that mercy was shown to a people outside of God's covenant people.

The first time the word 'judge' appears in the Bible is in Genesis 15:14. God promised to judge Egypt after the Children of Israel had been in bondage for four hundred years. And what happened? God sent 'plagues' upon Egypt. The first nine were mainly gracious judgements – warnings (Ex. 7–10). But the tenth, the killing of the firstborn, was wrath without mixture (Ex. 12:29–30). It was retributive judgement, as was the destruction of Pharaoh's army in the Red Sea (Ex. 14:27, 28).

The first time the word 'judgement' appears in the Bible is in Genesis 18:19. God showed Abraham what he would do to Sodom and Gomorrah – that they would be destroyed in flames. We must surely call that retributive judgement upon promiscuity.

And yet there is no sign that Sodom and Gomorrah were warned – or that God was angry. It was *silent* judgement followed suddenly by retributive judgement. When Abraham saw it coming he raised the question, 'Shall not the Judge of all the earth do right?' (Gen. 18:25).

Abraham's question is good for us to raise when we don't understand God's ways. Or when we don't understand eternal punishment, for example. We know it is in the Bible. But if we can't understand it, let our voices be lowered. Abraham didn't understand either, but he just said, 'Shall not the Judge of all the earth do right?'

There is another aspect of judgement which will bear our looking into. That is when God turns his judgement inwardly upon his own covenant people. When God said of the Children of Israel, 'I sware in my wrath, that they should not enter into my rest' (Psalm 95:11), it was simultaneously retributive and redemptive judgement. Although Israel belonged to the Lord, they grieved him. They were prohibited from inheriting the promised land as a consequence of their unbelief. This loss of inheritance was retributive but their sin did not cut them off from God's promise concerning the age to come.

That generation of Israel was a type of the Christian who is saved but who may none the less incur God's judgement. Certain Christians in Corinth were judged with 'premature' death. It was partly retributive (1 Cor. 11:30–32). And yet then Paul said that some of them were 'sickly' (v 30) this was gracious judgement as well; for they, as well as the rest of the church, were being warned.

At the time of Korah's rebellion against Moses retributive judgement followed; but it too became a warning: 'And the earth opened her mouth, and swallowed them up together with Korah, when that company died, what time the fire devoured two hundred and fifty men – and they became a sign' (Num. 26:10) ('Warning sign' says NIV). The rebellion brought about God's anger, yes, but it was gracious judgement.

God once sent a plague upon Israel for heterosexual promiscuity (Num. 25:9). Never think that God singles out the homosexual. In Numbers 25:9 we read, 'And those that died in the plague were twenty and four thousand.' But then the plague was stayed. Why? The survivors repented, and it turned out to be gracious judgement.

This pattern of gracious judgement, a mixture of retribution and mercy but always warning, is to be seen right through the Old Testament. It continues through the period of the Kings and the Prophets, and it must be said that it is the predominant kind of judgement seen in the Old Testament. It is often followed by mercy bestowed upon a repentant Israel.

I turn now to the present generation. It has to be said first that the lines between the covenant people of God and those outside this realm are not easily drawn. I make this point because of the stories above pertaining to Israel. Israel is a type of the church. Thus my referring to God turning 'inwardly' upon his own covenant people may cause one to ask, how might AIDS be a sign of God's judgement upon the church? When an alarming number of clergymen are reportedly inflicted with AIDS, one cannot but wonder whether God is not only judging society generally but also the church particularly. I do not know, if only because the lines between the church and the world are not too easily drawn – I am not sure that any one nation can be regarded as being under a special covenant, as Israel was.

Neither must we think that God is singularly angry with San Francisco, Africa, Haiti or the little town of Belle Glade in Florida, where you have the greatest concentration of the AIDS epidemic anywhere in the United States. At this writing, one person in fifteen has AIDS in San Francisco. One person in fourteen hundred in Great Britain. But the statistics change daily. At the present time one a day is dying of AIDS in Britain and we are not far from this figure becoming two a day. It is not known how many of those who have the HIV virus will develop AIDS. As we said above, twenty percent is presently regarded as the minimum, but the possibility is real that they will *all* eventually get it. It is estimated that four thousand people will die in Britain by 1990, and that the number of people currently infected in the United Kingdom is between forty and fifty thousand.

I raise again this question, why AIDS now? Why all of this now? Why not a thousand years ago? Why not a hundred years ago? Or fifty years ago? It seems to me that the answer lies in the interaction of two causes, (1) God's love for the world he made and gave his Son for (the underlying cause) and (2) the vast, unashamed promiscuity that finally went so far that the strain proved too great (the precipitating cause). The result: gracious judgement.

There might have followed an indefinite display of silent judgement; God doing nothing. Indeed, there may have been a fear for some that God would simply wink an eye at the 'swinging sixties' or the 'me decade' of the seventies. But no. I rather think that God looked down from heaven upon the world he loves and decided to inflict a plague that was so obviously connected to sexual promiscuity that the question of 'God's judgement' emerged *even among those* who had not really given God much thought before.

In our day the permissive society seems to have come into its own. The 1967 Sexual Offences Act opened the floodgates for a tide of promiscuity which MPs never envisaged at the time, although they should have. Now there are state schools that are teaching homosexual practice as an equally valid and normal way of life. The Gay and Lesbian Charter even recommends that civil protection or charitable status be withdrawn from any person or from churches who speak against homosexual practice. The emergence of the AIDS epidemic alongside the permissive society therefore is far from coincidental. So it is not silent judgement that we are seeing.

But what about natural judgement? I am sure that this is certainly part of the answer. But if AIDS is to be seen merely as the consequence of sin, why should this awful phenomenon only appear now? It seems to me that there must be more at work than the inevitable consequence of sin. Something as awful as AIDS suggests that a fairly strong signal is being issued from beyond. An article in *The Times* in November 1987 predicted that, unless a vaccine or a cure for AIDS is developed, the epidemic will not peak until the end of the next century. I therefore think that God has superimposed a grevious phenomenon upon the normal 'You reap what you sow' syndrome.

On the other hand, is AIDS God's retributive

judgement (getting even)? I don't think so. Why would he single out personal morality? Why does he not judge public morality? Why not the Mafia? Why not communism, or the unacceptable face of capitalism? On some evils one must say it may be that God's silent judgement is in operation. For God is 'slow to anger' (Ps. 103:8). In any case we must remember that the end is not yet. God let Israel suffer for four hundred years before he sent Moses.

In what sense then is AIDS the judgement of God? We can draw a conclusion by bringing together the Biblical categories of judgement, Romans 1, and also the prophets. We are compelled to ask what would the Old Testament prophets have said had AIDS or its equivalent come in their day? What do you suppose Joel would have said? Or Amos? Or what about Elijah? Certainly they would have seen such as a plague sent from God upon promiscuity.

Now Romans chapter 1 is a description of God giving people over to their choice of a way of life. They chose lust over the knowledge of God. Their punishment was getting to have their own way. I repeat, Paul puts homosexual promiscuity at the top of the list not because there is a hierarchy of sins, but because there is a hierarchy of shame. For homosexuality defies God's natural order of creation. God made us male and female. And Paul says they received the due penalty for their sins. They reaped what they sowed. So it was minimally the consequence of sin.

The one thing which ought to be obvious to the world is that AIDS is certainly a vindication of God. It is a vindication of the Bible. Whoever you are – whatever emotion you may be feeling, you surely see that the Bible has got it right. And all this talk about 'safe sex' – fewer partners, vetting your partners, the use of condoms – will *not* end the spread of AIDS. One should read what Dr Patrick Dixon has to say on the nature of the AIDS virus and the use of condoms. In a word 'Condoms are unsafe' (*The Trust About Aids*, pp 110–122).

I believe that the appearance of AIDS is to be best explained as God's *gracious* judgement. For AIDS to our society is like pain to a diseased body. But pain is a very gracious gift, because when you are ill but without pain you know nothing is wrong. The horror of cancer is that it begins painlessly. The pain only emerges in the advanced stages – but even then there is often hope! I therefore think there could still be hope for our society.

This is why I don't believe that the AIDS plague is a retributive judgement of God. I believe AIDS is his gracious judgement, that is, the consequence of gracious judgement upon promiscuity.

Some may ask, 'What about the innocent victims?' Sadly, they are to be seen as part of the inevitable fall-out of any great catastrophe which God allows to happen. Jesus hinted at this when he forecast Jerusalem's destruction in 70AD and said, 'Pray ye that your flight be not in the winter' (Matt. 24:20).

AIDS is the bitter token of gracious, not retributive, judgement. If it were retributive you would have to say there was no hope for anybody who had AIDS of being converted. And that would be to pronounce judgement while the jury is still out. That is not all; God may after all send a cure and a vaccine for AIDS through common grace.

But with this I come to a conclusion; the AIDS epidemic should be seen as a merciful warning, both

collectively and individually. Collectively, it could
change lifestyles. It hasn't done it yet, and I have to
admit there is little sign of it happening[1], but it could
signal an end to the permissive age. It could change
the lifestyle of millions. *Time* magazine has devoted a
cover story to this idea. In *The Daily Mail* this item
appeared in March 1987, 'In AIDS-conscious 1987
expect things to disappear – like films condoning
sexual promiscuity.' According to this writer,
'There is no chance for Percy, and a worried frown
for Valley of the Dolls. They say that even Cagney
and Lacey will change their lifestyle. Make no
mistake: old-fashioned morality is staging a come-
back, for practical reasons[2].'

All this coincides with what many medical people
have been saying for years – that cervical cancer is on
the increase and the real killer is sexual intercourse with
multiple partners. So the AIDS phenomenon is God
reaching out to a world he loves. Yes – he's angry. But
he cares. It might have been a silent judgement.

So what about the warning individually? It is
gracious judgement even upon those who unluckily
contract AIDS! For they know that they have only a
year or so to live. And if the reader of these lines has
AIDS you still have got time to heed the warning to
turn to Christ as your Lord and Saviour.

Could the AIDS phenomenon be redemptive
judgement? I answer, that is up to you. Because you
can turn all that has happened – that which is
gracious judgement – partly retributive, partly
merciful but always a warning – into redemption.
For it could be that you are now thinking of turning
to God when you wouldn't have any other way.

Allow me to put it like this. Suppose you have
AIDS. But you are converted to Christ because you

know your time is short. You die, you wake up in Heaven! Suppose it turns out that you did not get your three score and ten like most people. Perhaps this made you bitter at first. But not in Heaven! Dare I say it, you will then say, 'Thank God I got AIDS, for I turned to him. I wouldn't have otherwise. The way I was going nothing would have stopped me. It took AIDS to drive me to God.'

This is nothing new. We've all needed God's chastening at one time or another. When Jonah found himself in the belly of a great fish it is written: '*Then* Jonah prayed unto the Lord his God' (Jon. 2:1). When? 'Then'. But only then. We are all like that. 'For he knoweth our frame; he remembereth that we are dust' (Ps. 103:4).

[1]Dr Jonathan Mann of the World Health Organisation has warned the public against heterosexual complacency in the United States and Europe, where homosexual cases predominate. (*The Times*, 27th January 1988).

[2]Addressing the aforementioned World Summit on AIDS the Princess Royal called the AIDS epidemic a 'classic own goal by the human race', that it was a 'self-inflicted wound that only served to remind *homo sapiens* of their own fallibility'. In response an editorial in the *The Times* commended her right to insist that there is normal moral dimension to AIDS. By far the largest factor in its spread arises from patterns of voluntary sexual behaviour, and it is a moral imperative that these patterns must change. Anyone who refuses to heed the warning . . . risking not only his or her own health and life but that of thousands of others, many of whom will be children'. (*The Times* 25th January 1988.) A *Daily Mail* editorial (25th January 1988) likewise applauded Princess Anne's common sense.

Chapter Six

Why Become a Christian?

I am going to ask that we look one more time at Romans Chapter 1, verses 26–28:

> 'For this cause God gave them up unto vile affections: for even their women did change the natural use into that which is against nature: And likewise also the men, leaving the natural use of the women, burned in their lust one toward another; men with men working that which is unseemly, and receiving in themselves that recompense of their error which was meet. And even as they did not like to retain God in their knowledge, God gave them over to a reprobate mind, to do those things which are not convenient.'

Three times we find in Romans 1 the phrase, 'God gave them up.' So why did Paul say this? What is his point? What if this describes you? Suppose, as you were reading the above verses, you said to yourself, 'Well, that sounds an awful lot like me!' Yet it says, 'God gave them up.' You might conclude that God has therefore finished with you.

My answer to that is that God is letting you read

these verses and read this book in order that you might be warned. Whenever you read God's word or hear a word preached, and it puts you on the spot and makes you feel uncomfortable or condemned, your reaction may well be 'There's no hope for me.' But let me tell you, when you hear a word like that it means there *is* hope. Because if there were no hope God wouldn't even bother to give this word to you. God does not play games with our souls.

What we read above is an explicit reference to lesbianism and male homosexual practice. But maybe that is not your problem at all. For when God gives one over to a reprobate mind (Rom. 1:28) it is not because he has singled out a particular sexual sin or weakness. Not at all. The reprobate mind is one that is 'devoid of judgement'. It can no longer think clearly. And it may be that you are just like this. You are in confusion. There is no 'presence of mind'. Or you may feel that the situation in which you find yourself is one of despair, and you are just sure there is no hope for you.

I can tell you, that is the devil. The devil will always make you think that there is no hope, that there is no way out. Suppose you are afraid that you have got AIDS or some other disease. Well, there *is* hope for you.

In the previous chapter we looked at five categories of judgement which are found in Holy Scriptures. I must now repeat three of these. (1) Retributive judgement – where God gets even and punishes you for what you did. 'The wages of sin is death' (Rom. 6:23). Death is retributive judgement upon the human race because we sin. It is the only reason that people die. If you never sinned you would never die. So if you ever run into somebody who says that they never sin you ought to say, 'Congratulations – do you know you are never going to die?'

There is another kind of retributive judgement, and that is eternal punishment. That is when God shows how much he hates sin by allowing men to go to a place the Bible calls hell. There are other names for it. Jesus also called it 'outer darkness', where 'there shall be weeping and gnashing of teeth' (Matt. 8:12). Such retributive judgement has no end. (2) Gracious judgement, which is partly retributive (because God is angry), but is mainly warning (because there is hope). So if you sense God's anger it means indeed that God doesn't like what you have done. But he's stepping in and doing something about it! And it may not be because of sexual sin. Perhaps you are filled with greed, hate or a desire for vengeance. Maybe you have walked over people to get where you are, but now you are feeling awful. Gracious judgement is mainly a warning, and before we can be saved we must all experience what is called 'conviction of sin' (John 16:7). We suddenly feel in terror of the same sin we have been able to commit for a long time without it ever bothering us. We are in trembling and fear. This is God's gracious warning – but there is hope.

(3) Silent judgement. It is when God does nothing. And I have to say this. If you are one of those who has apparently been able to get away with sin, that's the worst sign of all. Because it's an ominous hint from God that he's just not going to deal with you in this life at all. There are those who do get away with murder – with robbery, adultery or with homosexual fornication. They walk over people to get to where they are. There are dictators of governments – ruthless politicians – they get away with everything,

and God does nothing. What does it mean?

It means silent judgement. God has just decided to wait and judge them later. It will be suddenly and without any further warning, when they will stand before God and have to give an account of the way they have lived. Jesus said, 'Marvel not at this: for the hour is coming, in which all that are in the graves shall hear his voice, and shall come forth; they that have done good unto the resurrection of life; and they that have done evil, unto the resurrection of damnation' (John 5:28, 29).

Silent judgement? Yes, for a while. But suddenly, without warning, all of us will have to give an account of our lives. Some will hear from Jesus himself the words, 'I never knew you: depart from me, ye that work iniquity' (Matt. 7:23). They will be consigned to a place where there is 'wailing and gnashing of teeth' (Matt. 13:50).

Let us suppose that you are beginning to fear God's judgement. Let us suppose that, suddenly, things are coming in on you and you are feeling hemmed in. You are suddenly uncomfortable – you have been found out.

Or perhaps somebody knows about you and you are living in shame and fear. The worst thing of all, you say, is that you have been found out. So what does this mean?

It is wonderful – the most wonderful thing of all. Because it is a sign that God *is* going to deal with you, and that there is hope. If you are feeling this conviction – you feel full of guilt and shame inside, and are afraid, and even running from God, I say this: God would not let you feel this way and dangle the threat of damnation before you and then say, 'There's nothing you can do.' The devil will say that.

But whoever you are, God would not have you read this if there was no hope.

You may feel that your particular situation is so intricate, involved and hopeless that you have even thought of suicide – any way to get out of this life. Because nothing you say can solve your problem.

Do you know what the Bible says? 'With God nothing shall be impossible' (Luke 1:37). My advice is admit to your sin and quit blaming everybody else. Don't blame your parents or society or that school-teacher. Don't blame that boss you had or that person in the office. Just say, '*I* am the culprit. *I* am in trouble.' Own your sin and come to God and say, 'I'm sorry.' Don't plead any good works you may have – I don't doubt that you could muster up one or two. Or many. But they won't help. They may give you a good feeling, but it's a false sense of security. Trust in your good works – whether it's your church membership or your baptism – and the devil will lure you to sleep with the belief that these works will help you.

But when you disown them and own your sin and say, 'God, I'm sorry,' you thus plead only the merit of the blood that Jesus shed on the cross, and you come only to him and receive him as your Lord and Saviour. If you do receive him I promise you that God will take your broken life and sew the pieces together and make you a trophy of grace. Because God can do anything.

About six months ago a man came to see me in the vestry. He had discovered the Lord for the first time in his life. He had been coming to our Thursday lunchtime services, and came into the vestry a broken man. His wife had left him, divorced him and he said, 'I don't blame her.' But he had become a Christian, and the interesting thing was that she had also become a Christian. But she couldn't believe that his conversion was real. The man did not think there was any hope, but we prayed together. And do you know – I married them! They were remarried. Yet there seemed no hope.

And God will do something great for you. You may think there is no way out. You may say, 'I have been so awful, and I'm so ashamed.' There is a verse in the Bible that says, 'I will restore the years which the locusts have eaten.' In the book of Joel there is a reference to God sending locusts upon the land as a judgement for the people's sins. But Joel said that if the people came back to God, God would restore the years that the locusts have eaten (Joel 2:25). God will take your life and reshape it.

I don't understand how it works, but he will even shape your past! My favourite verse is Romans 8:28, 'And we know that all things work together for good to them that love God, to them who are the called according to his purpose.' Once you become a member of God's family he takes your whole past on board and causes everything to fit into a pattern for good.

And that is what God will do with you. You are not going to be mocked. You need not be threatened. You are not to say, 'There's no hope for me.' The reasons we have this reference about God giving some up is that it might shake us up and let us see that there is hope. Paul later says that 'the goodness of God leadeth thee to repentance' (Rom. 2:46). So whatever your weakness or fear may be, no matter what you have done, remember that there is a strain running right through the Bible which goes like this, 'Harden not your hearts' (Ps. 95:8; Heb 3:8, 15; 4:7).

89

'If any man hear my voice, and open the door, I will come in to him, and will sup with him, and he with me' (Rev. 3:20).

But there is also a verse which says, 'Seek ye the Lord *while he may be found*, call ye upon him while he is near' (Is. 55:6). And the Lord is near. He is right there with you and he can be found. Don't wait until you die. After you die, you'll pray the prayer (below) I want you to pray now. But it will be too late then. Should you go to hell you will ask God for mercy (see Luke 16:23, 24). But it will be too late then.

Now how does God speak to us? Many ways. He can speak through creation (Ps. 19:1). He speaks through the conscience (Rom. 1:20). He speaks through the Bible and through preaching (1 Cor. 1:21). But I want now to show that he speaks through *chastening*. Chastening means 'to correct by punishment'. So it too is a kind of judgement. It is partly retributive in that God is angry and he steps in. You are found out and you feel pretty bad. But chastening is for our own good – for your correction.

There are three types of chastening; internal, external and terminal. Internal chastening is when you feel smitten in your heart and feel awful. And this is, by the way, the best way to have your problem solved. If you just listen to God's word, heed it and obey it, you can solve your problem at that level.

Another level is external chastening. Now why external? It is employed when internal chastening does not work. In other words, when you hear God speak but don't accept it, God has another way of reaching you. Jonah ran from God, but God sent a wind and a fish which swallowed up Jonah. This was external chastening. When God comes from without he may put you flat on your back. He may cause a financial reverse in business. He may withhold vindication from you. He may put you through sorrow – you may have to 'eat dust' for a while. God sometimes does what it takes to secure the response in us that he wants.

What is terminal chastening? It comes at the judgement seat of Christ. When certain Christians will be saved, to use Paul's word, 'so as by fire' (1 Cor. 3:15b). They will suffer 'loss'. Not loss of salvation but loss of reward in Heaven.

Now this matter of chastening, it seems, is something that actually applies only to the Christian. Therefore if you are truly chastened, it's a very good sign; because it means the Lord is after you! 'For whom the Lord *loveth* he chasteneth, and scourgeth every son whom he receiveth' (Heb. 12:6). Lamentations 3:39 says, 'Wherefore doth a *living* man complain, a man for the punishment of his sins?' If God is dealing with you while you are alive it's a fairly strong hint that he's not going to deal with you in hell. So if you are alive and are being punished, then get on your knees and say, 'Thank you God, for dealing with me in this way.'

Paul said, moreover, 'If we would judge ourselves, we should not be judged' (1 Cor. 11:31). That means that if you deal with yourself now, that is, deal with the problem and walk in the light that God gives you, you will 'not be condemned with the world'. For to be condemned with the world is to be dealt with at the judgement like all non-Christians. But when we *are* judged, it shows that we won't be condemned with the world. That means that God's intervening in our lives in the here and now means that we are being treated as his own.

Chastening therefore is for the Christian. But what if you are not a Christian? What if you are not only not a Christian but you have no plans ever to become one? I have to tell you what's out there in the future for you. There are three possibilities. The first is what I call *calamity*. In fact it's not my word, it is what Proverbs 1:26 says, 'I also will laugh at your calamity.' 'Because I have called, and ye refused; I have stretched out my hand, and no man regarded . . . I will also laugh at your calamity; I will mock when your fear cometh' (v.24, 26).

In the seventeenth century, the Puritan Thomas Brooks wrote a book called *Heaven on Earth*, in which he showed that God gives the Christian a little bit of heaven to go to heaven in. But do you know that God sometimes does the reverse of this to the wicked man who is not saved? God may give you a little bit of hell to go to hell in.

You may say to me, 'But I'm in hell now.' I had someone in the vestry once who said precisely that to me – and I can believe it. But that's *not* the hell the Bible is talking about, where there is 'weeping and gnashing of teeth'. For the hell described in the Bible is unending.

You may contract AIDS. You may be in another kind of trouble and be ashamed. Catastrophe may await you in this life. But God can laugh. And that may well mean it is too late. Have you heard the Gospel, but laughed and scoffed at it? The Bible says, 'My spirit shall not always strive with man' (Gen. 6:3).

You may say, 'Why are you talking like this to me?' I'll tell you why: because there is hope right now, and if you are not shaken – if you are not jarred to see the threat of damnation that awaits you in the future – you may never come to Christ. So the kindest thing I can do is to come to you on bended knee and say, 'Turn from your wicked ways. Turn to the Lord.'

The second thing which may await you in the future is *contempt*. In Psalm 147 there is a verse which reads like this: 'Who can stand before his (God's) cold?' (v 17). Do you know what that means? It is a reference to God's cold shoulder – where God doesn't both any longer to let you know his feelings. It is that silent judgement I've been talking about. God will just treat you with contempt. What is contempt? You show contempt for a person by not speaking to him or her, by having nothing whatever to do with them. So when God shows contempt he does just that. He doesn't bother with you, to warn you or awaken you. He doesn't judge you. Or even let you get caught. He lets you flourish until one day the third possibility will be yours.

The third possibility is *condemnation*. This means the final judgement. 'As it is appointed unto man once to die, and after that the judgement' (Heb. 9:27). It is graphically described in Revelation 20:11–15.

God has given to Jesus the authority to execute judgement. Jesus himself said, 'He that rejecteth me, and receiveth not my words, hath one that judgeth him: the word that I have spoken, the same shall judge him in the last day' (John 12:48). Now the Bible describes two comings of Jesus. The first was when Jesus was born of a virgin. Do not ever forget that God was the father of Jesus. The Holy Spirit – the third person of the Trinity – came to the virgin Mary and implanted her womb with the seed of God, called the *logos* (Greek); the *word* that in the beginning, 'was with God, and the Word was God.' 'And the Word was made flesh, and dwelt among us' (John 1:1, 14). Mary gave birth to the God-man. Jesus was God as though he were not man, and man as though he were not God. That was his first coming.

Thirty-three years later, after having lived a life without any sin, he ended up on a cross. He was crucified, he was buried, he rose from the dead, and forty days later he ascended to heaven. Ten days after that the Spirit came upon the disciples on the Day of Pentecost. For nearly two thousand years the Church has been in existence, while Jesus has been at the right hand of God.

But he is coming a second time. And when he comes the second time he will not come as a lamb, but as 'the Lion of the tribe of Judah' (Rev. 5:5). The Bible says, 'Behold, he cometh with clouds; and every eye shall see him, and they also which pierced him; and all kindreds of the earth shall wail because of him' (Rev. 1:7). On that day men will weep and wail and gnash their teeth at the sight of Jesus. And that is when you will stand before him. Your whole life will pass before you and you will even get an opportunity to defend yourself. You may plead the merit of your good works. You may say, 'Haven't I done a lot of good things?' But you need to know that the *only* thing which will save you will *not* be your works but the fact that *while you were alive* you put all of your trust in Jesus Christ, who died on the cross for your sins. Jesus put it like this, 'For as the Father raiseth up the dead, and quickeneth them; even so the Son quickeneth whom he will. For the Father judgeth no man, but hath committed all judgement unto the Son' (John 5:21, 22). And he also said – and this is the promise for you now – 'He that heareth my word, and believeth in him that sent me, *hath* everlasting life, and *shall not come* into condemnation; but is passed from death unto life' (John 5:24).

Those are the three possibilities before you if you have no plans to become a Christian. It is only a matter of time until you are going to stand before God, and the big question you have got to ask is, 'How can I avoid that condemnation?' Jesus said that you can pass from death unto life. It's called conversion. Something happens to you, and you are changed. Converted. It is always in the passive tense. You don't *convert* – you *are converted*. It's something God does. It's your only hope; that God should step down to where you are and awaken you and that you should recognise you are hemmed in and plead for mercy. Then you will pass from death to life.

Has God spoken to you in these pages? In reading this book have you heard from God? You must go through two stages. First, you must hear God's voice. Secondly, you must heed it. But you can't heed it until you have heard it. You know in your heart of hearts whether God has spoken to you.

The question is, what will you do now? I am going to ask you to do something. If you have heard God speak I want you to act upon it. Heed his voice and believe it. Believe what you have heard. And you can show that you believe it simply by uttering this prayer right there, wherever you are. You don't need to say it out loud, for you can say it in your heart:

Dear God, I need you. I want you. I know that I have sinned against you. I am sorry for my sins. Wash my sins away by Jesus' blood. I confess that he is the Son of God. I welcome your Holy Spirit into my heart. As best as I know how I give you my life. In Jesus' name.

Amen.

95